CW00665200

MICHAEL ROSEN'S POETRY VIDEOS: HOW TO GET CHILDREN WRITING AND PERFORMING POEMS TOO

JONNY WALKER
WITH
MICHAEL ROSEN

Contents

Introduction

Here's the summary of this book.

I am a teacher who loves poetry, and I'm going to share ways that you can create a rich poetry community with your children. We will do this by engaging with the enormous collection of videos on Michael Rosen's YouTube Channel – 'Kids' Poems and Stories with Michael Rosen.'

As a kid, I was obsessed with cheeky limericks and funny rhymes. As a teenager, I poured youthful angst into bad but intimate verse. As an adult, I teach poetry and get to share it with the kids.

The joy, understanding and frustration that poetry can engender is what makes me happy to be a teacher-writer. Ross Young and Felicity Ferguson, who run the Writing for Pleasure Centre, define a teacher-writer as someone 'who writes with and for pleasure, and uses [their] literate life as a learning tool in the classroom'. I love that.

I am a primary teacher based in Newham in East London. I run residential poetry retreats with children aged 9 to 11, from across East London, taking them out to the New Forest and the South Downs. I also teach poetry in schools on residencies, and run creative writing networks for primary and secondary students.

Running these writing projects with children has taught me that in class we are often too prescriptive and too tentative. We don't give children enough space for real self-expression. I run the retreats with

Adisa the Verbaliser, a particularly effervescent performance poet, and seeing how he teaches poetry swayed my thinking about what goes on in my classroom.

Given the time to have rich conversations together, children and teachers can find themselves – and each other – as writers. Given the encouragement to write from our interests and experience, everybody realises they have something to say and the right to say it. Given the proper time to think and edit, we can all produce writing that matters.

Under these conditions, the writing becomes more meaningful, enjoyable and social. Ideas become better-expressed. There is a greater desire to experiment with different forms and structures. Children develop tastes, knowing what they like to read, how they like to write, and how they like to share their work. The desire to perform grows organically from the pride in their writing.

We want poetry that captures our lives on the page – that makes us laugh, that makes us cry, that makes us smile, that makes us think. We want poetry that can be playful and serious, poetry that can be tamed and poetry that can be wild.

One of the most powerful exponents of this poetry is Michael Rosen.

His poetry is funny, accessible to children, and grounded in real life. It is sometimes playful and sometimes serious. It sometimes rhymes and sometimes doesn't. It is sometimes true, and sometimes not. It never shies away from important discussions. It doesn't patronise or discriminate.

Michael's YouTube channel 'Kids Poems and Stories with Michael Rosen' is a treasure trove, and an asset to us as teachers of Literacy and English. It contains hundreds of videos, going back to the days before YouTube went mainstream. It is a live archive, still growing each week.

When I was Children's Laureate from 2007 to 2009, I made an effort to work with people who could video children doing poetry in schools, and we spoke about starting a channel. My son Joe is a video-maker and  he filmed me performing a few poems and put them on YouTube. We ignored it for a few years, and then came back and we were like "Oh look! Goody! We've got thousands of subscribers!" so we built on that. Now we have well over half a million subscribers and over 100 million views.

Going around schools and talking to teachers, they had tended mostly to look at just a few of the videos – maybe 'Bear Hunt' or 'Chocolate Cake'. I thought it would be good if teachers had a bridge between the straight entertainment of the YouTube channel and their own practice in helping children to write.

That's why this book came about. I approached Jonny because I wanted the book to be written by a practising teacher. It's all very well for me to sit on my high horse and say 'you could go to the woods for three hours looking at moths' but that might not be the reality day-to-day for teachers.

We teachers probably know about the video performances on the channel of 'Chocolate Cake' and 'Strict' and 'We're Going On A Bear Hunt'. We probably don't all know about 'On The Move Again', 'Newcomers' and 'My Brother Is On The Floor Roaring'.

There are poems, songs, stories, workshops, interviews and even beatboxing tutorials!

When Michael asked whether I would like to collaborate on a book for teachers, guiding them about how to use his YouTube channel in creative ways, I leaped at the chance. Partly, this is because I am a horrendous fanboy of his, and partly this is because I truly believe that this book has the potential to transform the way we teach poetry.

In the lockdown that began in March 2020, when most children in the UK found themselves learning from home, the potential of a safe YouTube-linked approach to teaching poetry became even clearer.

This handbook should help you to embrace the full potential of a poetry writing classroom; one that rattles to the rhythm of Rosen, whether we are teaching in person or online. Use Michael's videos to help you teach vibrant lessons which firmly locate self-expression at the heart of your classroom.

Talking to teachers and to my own students about poetry, I came up with a list of eight of the most interesting and commonly-asked questions. These questions form each of the first eight chapters in Part One.

Part Two has a different format. It is simply a conversation I had with Michael over Zoom, talking about why any of this matters.

This is a practical book, designed to be used, not just read. Keep it next to you as you are planning your English lessons. Get it grubby and tattered. Try things out. Let it sit in your backpack, amongst all the confiscated toys and bits of paper we somehow accumulate every day.

Most of the time in this book, it will be me talking to you, but I have the unusual privilege of being able to summon Michael Rosen to our chat. When we get stuck, or whenever he wants to pop up and challenge me . . . *BOOM* . . . he will arrive.

Michael, how do you want to be positioned in this book? The expert? The guide on the side? The poetic genie?

Possibly as a bit of a cheat. I can do something that you can't, which is specialise only in poetry. I can walk about thinking about poems, about books I've written, and about performing poetry – you've got to teach Maths and Geography and a hundred other things. I can offer my specialised thoughts. I went to university and studied poetry and have been studying it ever since. Since I'm an old geezer that's quite a lot of years to have been thinking about poetry. When teachers like you ask questions, I can draw on 55 years of playing with this stuff.

Each of the following chapters is a mix of discussion, reflection and activities around eight interesting questions about teaching children to write and perform poetry.

The activities are clear mini-lessons that you can easily build into your teaching. Each mini-lesson refers to Michael's videos on the channel. Each one explains how we can guide children to understand how poetry works, and how we can help them create their own.

All of the videos I refer to are on the channel. Whilst you could just search for them individually by poem title on YouTube, we have also set up Playlists for you, which list the videos in the order they appear in this book.

Helpful aren't we?

Give the children a notepad for them to jot down their thoughts and to write their poems. This is different from an exercise book, which is collected in and belongs to you as the teacher. The notepad is where they can test things out and develop their ideas. It can be private to them. They can choose to 'let you in' – and they usually do – but they are the gatekeepers of their own writing.

Really take the time to talk. I know that sounds obvious, but time is everything, and rushing helps nobody.

Let the ideas percolate. We often cut out the time for this, instead prioritising the filling in of planning grids and such like. Talk is planning, and through conversation, we can develop our ideas and understanding.

Ideally, this guide will empower you to open the door to poetry with your children, to always keep it ajar, and to go through it yourselves too, pen in hand.

It can help us teachers to resist the pressure to sap the life out of poetry. The way in which reading is assessed in the SATS can lead to poems being reduced to husks and specimens. We hollow out the meaning and the ambiguity alike. We ignore personal responses, searching for a 'correct answer' to soulless questions that needn't be asked in the first place.

In its own quiet way, writing and performing poetry in the way we describe in this book is a defiant act. It values children's own authentic voices and it values ours as their teachers. In the way we explore and unpick Michael's videos, we are celebrating what can be achieved when we take the time to talk, share experiences and connect with each other through a love of words.

And paradoxically enough, through doing this, we develop children's ability to write well, which is precisely what the constrained curriculum strives fruitlessly to achieve.

You'll see a change in yourself and your children when you start to realise your capabilities. You become a 'Can Do' person. Poetry doesn't feel constraining, and it can feel like you are free to engage with it at any level. If you have a three-year-old you will hear them engage in poetry as wordplay. I saw a child dancing around a little dome in Brighton, and as she danced she made up a little song that went 'Dancey, Dancey, Dancey – I am dancing.' She felt free to make a poem and she did it. She didn't need to go to university to learn how to do it, she just knows it is something that gives her pleasure. Ideally we can all be like that.

Education is always political, and the practicalities of teaching poetry in school can be challenging; children's freedom, self-expression and creativity are not equally valued by everybody.

So let's seize the flame and embrace poetry for the fabulous, writhing hotbed of contradictions that it is. Teachers, grab your quills. Michael, I've got you on speed dial.

To the classroom we go!

PART ONE

1　Does It Need To Rhyme?

'I like poems because they rhyme'. You'll hear this pretty much every time you ask a child what they like about poetry. The National Literacy Trust's 2018 research 'A Thing That Makes Me Happy' asked the question to over 2000 pupils, and 'rhyming' was by far the most common answer.

Children often don't just think that poetry *contains* rhymes; they think that poetry *is* rhymes. This is a starting point that we need to account for when we are building up children's familiarity with poetry – ask your own children and see what they say.

You can see why they might perceive it this way. Most of the poetry they first encounter is in the form of nursery rhymes, songs and chants, and rhythmic rhyming verse in picturebooks.

This is not the end of the world. It's not even a bad thing. It is a simple enough task to show them other forms of poetry that do not need to rhyme. But it is fair to say that the insatiable desire to rhyme can be a problem when children are still developing their vocabulary.

Rhyme is very attractive. It is almost seductive. We live in a culture where you might describe it as a 'front-running form'. If you think of song and rap and nursery rhymes and adverts and picturebooks . . . rhyme is one of the main forms. It's very attractive because it has this effect of chiming – you can almost predict the word that's coming once you have the pattern of the rhyme.

It is hard for children to tell something that feels true to them in rhyme. It may do, and I don't want to diminish any of the fun that you can have playing with rhyme, I do it all of the time – we'll come back to that – but if they are writing about what feels like a true experience to them, something that upset them or was really funny that their sister or brother said to them, then sometimes it's quite nice to play with the spoken sound of the language as opposed to the words that fit simply or only because they rhyme.

Children can lose sight of meaning out of a desperation to shoehorn in any word that rhymes. Sometimes a lack of truth is fine – they are sharing poems after all, not witness statements – but often they *intend* to tell a true story, but become derailed by rhyme.

How can we show children that poems don't always need to rhyme?

The simplest and most enjoyable way to unpick children's conflation of poetry with rhyme is to shower them with a flurry of different forms of poetry, and to do so regularly.

We can focus them on the importance of the story. A great poem doesn't necessarily need to rhyme if it tells a fascinating story, and tells it well.

The Outside Toilet

'The Outside Toilet' is a great example of a non-rhyming and non-rhythmic poem.

Share the poem with the children, and ask them to tell you what they learn from it. What do they learn about Michael? What do they learn about his family?

'The Outside Toilet' introduces several of the Yiddish words spoken around him when he was a child, and this is the setting for a tale of family, about the fear of the outside toilet, the movements of spiders and the desperate run through the dark to get to the light.

Encourage children to talk about running through the dark. Do they do this? Do they do anything similar, like run up the stairs when it is bedtime? From this talk, encourage them to tell each other their story like 'The Outside Toilet'. Encourage them to tell two other people. Then, encourage them to write it down, trying to write it exactly as they told it to their classmates.

For some children, this will be giving space to share their home languages on the page too. The fact that many multilingual children never have the chance to share their other languages is a missed opportunity to value the children's whole selves.

Valuing and welcoming children's 'actual' spoken language into the poetry classroom enables all children to share the dialects, slang and joyful jargon that are part of their everyday vocabulary. Children's social language draws on YouTube, memes, viral humour, TV, older siblings and gaming, just as much as it draws on dialect, spoken languages and family phrases. In amongst this richness, they don't need to worry about rhyming.

Another example from the channel could be 'The Register'.

'Be The Teacher' Poem

Ask the children whether they think there is such a thing as 'teacher language'. What sorts of things do teachers say? Ask them whether they think they could tell if someone was a teacher by the way that they spoke.

Share the poem 'The Register' in which the poem is the teacher's words as they take the class register. Children won't even need to be told the title to know exactly what is happening here. From Michael's very first words "Right Class 6", they know and recognise the situation. It is the intonation, the interjections and the shared jokes that entice the young poetry-absorbers, and sets their heads nodding.

Encourage the children to pretend to be the teacher, doing the register for their class. Let them write as the kind of teacher they would imagine themselves to be. How would their character be shown through their registration style?

This writing-in-role should make it easier for more reluctant writers to get started too. If it helps, you could get them to act out the scenes before they begin making notes and writing.

Children are alarmingly well-attuned to the talk of the school. They recognise the imploring tone of the tired teacher and the grandstanding of the new headteacher, and can put it down on the page. Likewise, they can mimic the mannerisms of their friends and classmates, and can write about this evocatively, without depending on rhyme.

Sometimes the things children say to each other are poetry in themselves.

On a Year 5 poetry retreat I led, I woke up one of the groups of children and was alarmed by what I saw when the door opened. One boy was looming aggressively over another, who looked as if he had just been attacked.

When he saw me, the shocked loomer staggered backwards and uttered the immortal phrase,

"But sir . . . It was only a light headbutt!"

They all immediately began laughing, and it turns out they had been caught out playfighting. Once it was clear no harm was done, I told him that his next poem could begin with that phrase, and his friends immediately crowded him and his notebook whilst he wrote this.

Excuse Poem

But sir!
It was only a light headbutt.

But sir!
It was only three punches.

But sir!
It was only a backhand slap.

But sir!
It was only pinching someone.

But sir!
It was only poking an eye.

Sir.
I have more excuses.

— *Ismaeel, Year 5, Vicarage Primary, Newham*

This is very exciting and I think what Ismaeel has done is create his own form. We've got repetition with 'But Sir! It was only', and he has found a way to mock himself with an inbuilt chorus. And we've got the 'But Sir!' which is him arguing with you, and 'it was only', when it was clearly not 'only'. There is irony and satire in it, which comes unstated, and that's what's clever about it.

In many of Michael's narrative poems just as in this spontaneous headbutting poem, the quality of the poem is in the quality of the story. It is about sharing the details that crystallise a moment. No rhyme is needed.

But how do we show children how to rhyme well if they are going to do it?

We don't want to go too far the other way and *dissuade* them from ever rhyming. Sometimes, we want to be able to rhyme, and we want to be able to do it well.

Children, by no fault of their own, haven't lived as long as adults. They have not typically picked up as much vocabulary as us.

Rhyming needs to coexist with meaning. It needs to make sense.

This doesn't mean that whatever they write about needs to have happened, of course, and it can be nonsensical too – it needs to make sense *as a story*. Nobody has declared The Jabberwocky to be fake news because of a lack of forensic evidence. Carroll's poem endures because the story is strong, the humour is subtle and the language is rich.

Pantomime Rhyme Poems

'Fast Food' is a good one to look at here.

Watch the video of Michael performing the poem. The story unfolds as Speedy Hamburger gets further and further away from the fryer, whilst the line of those pursuing him grows like in a pantomime.

> A hamburger sat in a hamburger bar
> waiting to be fried
> "No one's going to put me" it said,
> "into anyone's inside."
>
> "Eating me is cruel;
> eating me is murder.
> You can't catch me
> I'm The Speedy Hamburger."

To develop children's ability to piece their rhymes together, get them to create their own versions of this last verse. If not 'The Speedy Hamburger', who else could be running away? A Beastly Breadroll? A Violent Corn Cob? Let them struggle to create a version – they may struggle to think of foods which rhyme with negative words, such as 'cruel' or 'murder'.

Let this poem be an instructive struggle and work together to create versions that keep to the story whilst also rhyming.

> Eating me is bad
> Eating me is awful
> You can't catch me
> I'm the posh-voiced waffle.

Unlike Michael's anecdotal poetry about his childhood, 'Fast Food' isn't – unless I am really misreading it – designed to convey a deep meaning.

It is about the frivolous fun of poetry as play, and just as a game needs rules and structure, so does a rhyming story about a fleeing meat patty.

Any thoughts Michael? I hope I haven't desecrated your patty.

Well, if we go back to Lewis Carroll's 'The Jabberwocky', if you look at 'Twas Brillig', what was being parodied? It is the Great Adventure – the Great Battle. The Great Battle where you face the monster and then come home, into my arms my frabjous boy. But it is mocking it because it uses the heroic form but then undermines it by using nonsense words. With my one I was wanting to do something a bit similar. There's this heroic hamburger.

That in itself is just nuts isn't it – how can you have a heroic hamburger? But by animating it, personifying it, you can create something fun. At the same time it has a jokey or serious message about freedom, and so there is the idea that the hamburger can escape. You can use a formal shape of poem that has echoes of something grander than it is, and then diminish it by writing about something silly.

It's bathos. Children get that immediately.

A very simple and practical strategy to support children can be to produce a list of associated words which relate to the theme of their poem. They can then make a second list of words which rhyme with these associated words.

If they were writing about love, their first list might feature 'heart', 'emotion', 'care' and 'feelings'. Their rhymes might feature 'art', 'devotion', 'there' and 'ceilings'.

If they were writing a weird poem about dogs taking over a supermarket, their rhyme lists might help them to link their poodles with their noodles, their whining with their dining and their piddle with their Lidl.

Rhyming dictionaries can help with this, and there are plenty of online versions freely available too.

I use rhyming dictionaries and Roget. Particularly if I'm trying to write something difficult. The only snag that a teacher would have to watch is the tendency that kids get into for thinking that the message we are giving them is 'more words is better' in a poem.

In principle, rhyming dictionaries, Roget and the dictionary are great places to go. It's different ways of thinking. After all, a dictionary tells you what it means, Roget tells you lots of similar things, and a rhyming dictionary says these words sound similar. There's three different things and they're all on the computer anyway so you can just tap and get 'em.

It is sometimes really helpful to explore poems with children to help them to see where the rhymes are. Children can often think that rhymes live only at the end of a line, and can miss the playfulness and impact of internal rhymes – rhymes within the line.

Here is an example from one of my own poems about a boy who yawns on a lawn.

> But now he's forlorn
> Cos his plans have been torn
> From his hands and he's sworn
> He will stand on the lawn
> Eyes askance and he'll yawn
> On the lawn.

'Plans', 'hands', 'stand' and 'askance' all rhyme, (or they sort-of-do when I say them, at least).

When it comes to editing, the simplest form can be asking children whether the poem they have made does what they want it to do. Typically they want it to rhyme and to tell something; if it does one but not the other it is not quite there yet.

To illustrate this point, you can get the children to consider Michael's poems – does 'Chocolate Cake' suffer from not rhyming? No, of course not, it's not that kind of poem. Does 'The Michael Rosen Rap' benefit from its rhyming? Of course, it is that kind of poem.

How do we create brilliant poetry that does not rhyme?

In another booklet in this series, *Poetry and Stories For Primary And Lower Secondary Schools,* Michael describes poetry for children as 'a bridge between the oral and the written', and makes the point that 'what can be spoken, can be written'. This is worth bearing in mind when encouraging children to write poetry without rhymes.

Their poetry does not always need to be about deep philosophical ruminations on the human condition – by getting children to see their writing as part of living, they realise that they all have lots to say, and all the tools they need to say it.

And the irony of this is that children's most authentic poetry, when it is rich with their blunt, honest, mundane expressions of life, can very often end up ringing with a deeper universal meaning.

The topics we encourage children to write about can be chosen to harness their wealth of experience. Michael's book *Did I Hear You Write* shares a long list of the components of a young person's culture. This might include things like aspirations, friendship, rivalry, fears, music, and playground rhymes, but also memes, gaming and

YouTube. We have put together an updated list for 2021, which is included as an Appendix.

We don't lose anything by encouraging children to draw on what they know when they are writing. It is surely only schoolchildren and hard-up ghost-writers who are ever forced to write expressively with false passion about things they don't care about. We can help children to write with authenticity, with or without rhyme.

2   Does It Need To Be Serious?

Michael, I feel like I need you already on this one. When I was a kid, I saw most poetry as being quite lofty and obtuse. I saw it as being a bit posh and inaccessible.

My old English Lit teacher would get a twinkle in his eye when he read parts of The Canterbury Tales aloud to us, raising his eyes to suggest a secret meaning that kept passing me by.

At the time, this made me think that 'proper' poetry was fascinating but was also some kind of alchemy I couldn't quite understand. Have you found that many people bring misconceptions to poetry? Do other people see it as elite and serious, or is this my own personal hang-up?

I think most people's experience of poetry in the upper school and even at university is that analysing poems is a form of mild humiliation. Somebody or other knows more about this poem than I do. That's the feeling that you can have, so that either there is a critic who knows more about it than you, or that the teacher in front of you does. It may well be that the teacher themselves has had the same experience, that they've been humiliated at school or university. There's a weird cycle of learning-bashing that goes on, which we inflict on people down through the centuries. And it's a great shame because the whole point about poetry is that . . . it seems mad really . . . but poetry is written in order to be accessible.

One way I describe poetry is as being full of hooks. These hooks are what poets spend hours trying to put into poems, in order to hook the reader. And then we go to study these poems and instead of these hooks pulling you in and you're enjoying it, you are then told that you don't get it, or you don't know why it is effective. We are asked to explain why it is effective . . . what if we don't think it is effective?

One way to help is to do some groundwork before even reading the poem. Some of the best groundwork is to get kids talking or writing about a subject and then plopping the poem into the discussion. Shelley's Ozymandias is not a terribly easy poem, but if you get the kids talking about statues and self-importance and death, then the talk and the understanding of the poem will be richer.

Perhaps you – like me – bring your own perceptions and some misconceptions to the poetry classroom? The same is probably true of our pupils. Some will have a lovely relationship with it already. Some might be intimidated by it.

A good starting point with any class might be to unpick what they think poetry is. This will likely be a vibrant and interesting discussion in its own right, but can also be the foundation of some better-informed teaching from us.

Poetry can be about farts in the changing rooms. It can be about the dance of a crisp packet in the playground. It can be about our secret feelings. It can be about fascism, war, suffering and injustice. It can be all of these things.

Poetry does not *need* to be serious in its content, but it deserves to be taken seriously as a form. As teachers, we need to give children the time to discover its versatility.

We need to allow poetry to be more than just 'the thing we do when we've finished the term's fiction and non-fiction units', squeezing it in around Santa's classroom invasion and the End of Year parties. We need children to have time to read and write the fullest range of poetries.

Is everything worthy of poetry?

Seriousness can be tied to 'worthiness'.

Are all topics 'worthy' of being written about poetically? Can poetry help to capture the mundane experience of struggling to tie your shoelaces just as well as it can capture the hopeless desperation of star-crossed lovers? Can it help to express the emotions of a child who is enraged by a Fortnite feud as well as it can put voice to the feelings of a whole population in a moment of national reflection?

I reckon so. Poetry is the sponge that can absorb all human experience.

More than any other form, poetry enables child writers to share personal things. They should feel able to put their real thoughts down onto paper and do so in the knowledge that their ideas, jokes, anecdotes and experiences will be engaged with and considered respectfully by their classmates. It's a creative community.

As Michael writes in *What Is Poetry?*, this kind of writing 'has the advantage of allowing a reader or listener to think about whether they are anything like the people in the poem.' (p41).

In our classrooms, where children are relating to each other as classmates as well as writers, this takes on additional significance. It can help to deepen friendships and to understand differences. And understanding the lives of other people through their writing can help us to understand their behaviours too.

Family Talk

Consider anecdotal poems like Michael's 'Bubbe and Zeyde', which shares stories of childhood visits to his grandparents.

Tell the children that sometimes, a poem can be a way of 'letting someone in' to your own life. In the poem we will watch, Michael takes us back to his family when he was a child. Watch it.

In sharing details of the interactions between his mother and grandmother, and details of walks on Hackney Downs, think about how much we learn about Michael not just as 'the poet Michael Rosen' but as a living breathing human being.

Ask the children to jot down things that they have learned about his family, and ways in which his memory is similar or different to their own family life.

Getting children to engage with Michael's videos as a viewer and as a responder can help them to see how communicative a good poem can be. You could do the same process with many other poems on the channel.

Games and Mistakes

Show the children 'The Watch' to hear about how a game of 'Smugglers and Customs' broke his new wristwatch. What do your children discover about Michael, his friends and his family through this poetic story? What do you learn about the relationship between him and his brother?

Encourage the children to talk about and then write about a time that a game they were playing went wrong. Get them to switch between telling the story and writing the story so that they notice which bits are more interesting to different listeners.

Or you could show them 'Cold Pickles, Warm Chutney and Hot Jam'. Consider how much of a picture is painted about Michael's home through this poem about the smells in a corridor.

And you can do the same with the poetry your children write. If children are happy to share, let them do so and discuss together how much we learn about them through their poem stories.

When children are able to write candidly about their actual feelings and experiences it enables us to engage with their writing not as a form of assessment, quality assurance or evaluation, but as a form of connection, relating and bonding.

I can think of few outcomes more worthwhile than this. It is fascinating to see how the dynamics in a classroom can change when children and adults are relating with each other as appreciators of each other's writing. It has completely changed how I teach.

If we can take the anecdotal seriously, we can also take the universal seriously.

We can support children to read and write poetry that sharpens their social consciousness and gets them to think analytically about the forces that shape our society. It can be a way to focus in on challenging topics that are hard to discuss in the abstract.

Poetry steps into the world to look at it, rather than retreating away from it.

Poetry has always had a role in social and political change, and if we want to do more than pay lip service to children's rights and agency, then we should welcome discussions about social and political issues into our poetry classrooms.

In their book *Real-World Writers*, Ross Young and Felicity Ferguson argue for the importance of these kinds of poetry writing in the primary school classroom. 'Writing political and protest poetry is important because it gives children a way of expressing their feelings and worries, asking questions about the world and their dreams and hopes for the future . . . using their voice for social change can feel empowering and maybe even a little reassuring.' (p182)

'These Are The Hands', from the Michael Rosen for Adults channel, defends and celebrates the NHS. 'Fascism' warns of the pervasive creeping presence of authoritarianism. Poetry can help us to challenge pernicious forces in our society, and it can be a vehicle for us to articulate our values.

In times of crisis children can be given the chance to write in response to it. They will have a lot on their minds.

Life and Death

Ask the children whether they think a poem can help them to have difficult conversations. Let them know that one of the biggest taboos we have is death – it is something we find hard to talk about, even though it is a natural part of life.

Share the poem 'Today; One Day' a poem in which Michael talks of how 'today' may feel like everything has died, but that 'one day' those same things may feel different.

Try not to sway the mood by talking too much around the poem before watching – instead, watch it a few times, and perhaps give children time to talk. Why do they think Michael wrote this? What does it make them think of?

With some classes and some pupils, this might open a space to talk explicitly about grief, and with others, it may instead lead to discussion about optimism and the hope that things can better.

Encourage children to borrow from Michael's structure, contrasting 'todays' with 'tomorrows' or 'but one days'.

You can experiment with the sequence of discussion and poetry. If you start with discussion of an issue such as war or loss or equality, then the children's writing can be a more considered response to the issue; if you start with the poetry, then the discussion can be enriched by the children's more raw and instinctive responses, contained in their verses.

We need to be bold enough to facilitate a space for proper talk in our classrooms.

Our knowledge of our children should determine our choices. Not all children have the privilege of considering things like racism, war and refugeedom just as an abstraction. In our text choices and lesson plans, we should be mindful of how a child would feel if they had experienced the things we will teach about. The last thing one refugee child may wish to see is a depiction of the worst journey of her life, whereas another may be comforted by the chance to tell her story.

In introducing 'serious' topics into our discussion in a poetry classroom, we need to be equally serious about how we facilitate them. We need a classroom defined by the quality of its listening as much as the quality of its writing, in order for children's authentic views to surface and develop.

Sometimes, all that needs to be done to set the writing in motion is to share poetry on the themes being explored, and let discussion bubble up, as children have access to their notepads.

To give the example of racism, Kwame Alexander's 'The Undefeated' and Victoria Adukwei-Bulley's 'This Poem Is Not About Parakeets' are both examples of poems which pupils will be able to relate and respond to, whether or not they are drawing on personal experiences of it. Most will.

All topics are worthy of poetry, from intensely personal anecdotes to universal observations, from the daily grind to social and political change and everything that lies between.

Is poetry just confusing, florid and terrifying?

Poetry can be scary if we are only familiar with prose. This may be familiar.

What does this poem even mean, Miss?

There isn't just one meaning, Aaminah. That's the beauty of poetry.

But . . . what does it actually mean though?

What do you think?

I don't know Miss. Can't you just tell us?

Poetry looks, sounds and feels different to prose. It isn't just about rhyme and rhythm, but a particular kind of noticing.

This video, titled 'Why I Play Poetry' by Glenworth Primary, is a good example of this – when the children are talking about mixing paint and a football flying through the air, they are talking about so much more. About freedom, and play, and life.

Through the small details we see the bigger picture. The ambiguity is what gives it its authority and 'seriousness', not what detracts from it.

Exploring the language of poetry is all about basking in the shadow of doubt.

3　Does It Have To Be Funny?

Children find poetry funny.

This is because much of the poetry shared with them is designed to make them laugh, but it isn't just that. The toying with taboo, the exaggeration and repetition, the prodding at social norms and the eccentricity of performance are all part of the same humorous package.

Michael is a great example of all of this. Whilst his poetry is often written in order to make children laugh, it is not just the words themselves that achieve that aim. When he came to my school, he only needed to walk into the assembly and raise his eyebrows in order to fill the hall with uproarious peals of laughter.

You cannot dissect a poem to find the source of the humour. Rather than it being a thing, it is often the combination of many elements all woven together. It can be the fusion of surrealism, exaggeration, nonsense words and funny sounds, the wide-eyed performance and the child's ability to relate the story to their own experiences.

It can be the poet themselves that is funny, irrespective of what they do or say. The same is probably true in your classroom. Each class often has a few pupils who reliably make the others laugh, and the expectation of future laughs is always there.

Children's poetry does not *need* to be funny. Poetry for children often is, though, and if we want to lead a classroom that values the writing and performing of poetry, then we can often take the presence of laughter as a fairly good marker of how it is going.

How To Make Children Laugh

If you want to know more about Michael's views on how to make children laugh, he has helpfully written a book called *How To Make Children Laugh*.

For us here, it is useful to think about the role that humour plays in children's lives, and about what might happen if we give it a bit more of our attention.

I'm not dogmatic about that. I think I've been in classes where there haven't been many jokes and they've been absolutely terrific. I worked in a class where there weren't that many jokes but the work and the concentration and the creativity was incredible. Just because I'm keen on humour doesn't mean that I have to come and inflict that, either with my jokes or somebody else's, on everybody.

Understanding humour can help us to find the books that will get children hooked on reading. It can help us to plan writing lessons that are productive and enjoyable. It can help us to recognise the way that fear, power and laughter relate, and how that might feel for the children we teach. Funny poetry also needs to be taken seriously.

Let's talk about Strict

What makes Strict funny?

First up, watch 'Strict'.

It is a great one to watch with the children, first of all just for them to enjoy, and for you to see how it makes them laugh. Talk to them about which parts they seemed to find most funny, and ask them whether they have experienced anything similar.

This conversation alone is likely to help back up the idea that humour rarely sits far away from pain. Amongst their discussion of what is funny about it, you will likely hear talk of rules, power and a fear of 'getting caught'.

Encourage the children to tell their own stories of times when they were younger when they thought they might get in trouble. Perhaps, like Michael, they can tiptoe into exaggeration.

Let's unpick anxiety, surprise, absurdity and language-play in the context of Strict.

We know the *anxiety* of having to follow unreasonable rules, and the fear of what happens if you don't. The poem alludes to the fear of harm and death in the school prison. Michael, the survivor, sets himself apart from the weak and the whining, sniggering at the plight of his classmate Dave. It is the classroom as Darwinian battle.

There are plenty of *surprises* too. What begins as a seemingly true story about a teacher who *says* "No Breathing" quickly becomes one in which the rule is very much enforced. As we adapt to the shock of having to step over the bodies of deceased classmates, we then get blindsided by the reality of a three-week dangle in school prison.

It is artfully *absurd*, the layers of farcical horror nestled amongst the mundaneness of classroom conversations between teachers and the children. The class of 48 quickly becomes a class of 5, as the wily snatch a covert gasp of breath from inside their desks.

And there is *language-play* aplenty, especially in the way the words are performed by Michael. The 'ka-pum, ka-pum' sounds of collapsing children surround us. The kids watching the video imagine *their* classmates falling away beside them. The polite speech conventions of "But Miss . . . " sit incongruously amongst this everyday carnage.

Why does it make the children laugh then? Our children aren't used to this level of barbarism in their classrooms. But sitting beside the invented fear of a teacher insisting on no breathing, there is children's very real fear of the other rules that are insisted upon by us teachers.

"You can go to the loo in three mins, it'll be breaktime then," we tell the polite child reasonably, not recognising that they have been silently holding in a wee for 90 minutes and are worryingly close to the social death of wetting themselves.

Thinking of these four elements of humour is a strong starting point to getting children to write authentically from their experiences.

Anxiety, Surprise, Absurdity and Wordplay

Share some of the funny videos from the channel with your class. Encourage them to unpick together whether each video features anxiety, surprise, absurdity and/or wordplay. Particularly good choices for this activity would be 'A Whale Got On My Bus', 'Down Behind The Dustbin – Wayne' or 'Keith's Cupboard'

And when, later on, your children have written poems that they intend to be funny, perhaps they might want to analyse them in a similar way? Doing so can celebrate what they have been able to put together, whilst also highlighting ways they might experiment with it to make it funnier.

Children's Humour and Adults' Humour

Go with me on this strange anecdote.

I returned into our writing classroom after popping out to use the toilet, and a boy sitting closest to the door quietly feigned indignation.

"And *where* have you been, Sir?"

"Well I hardly think that's any of your business, young man . . . oh no I just kidding, I ran away to do peepee."

We laughed.

The humour for me was in the fact that he had enquired as to my whereabouts in a way that reversed the power dynamic.

The humour for him was the risk of making a personal joke, and his surprise at me breaking from my normal interaction to become exaggeratedly hostile, and then to switch into toddler talk.

Just because we are all laughing at the same time, it doesn't mean we are all laughing at the same thing.

Many of the best comedic children's stories and poems are so popular because they create different layers of humour. Knowing what makes our children laugh can be powerful knowledge when it comes to building learning relationships through creative writing.

What children find funny is not necessarily what we find funny. It is not necessarily what we think they will find funny. And it is often more nuanced than what we give them credit for.

Exaggeration

You could write a book about all the different elements of humour in children's writing. Michael has.

Since that book exists I'll not go into lots of detail, but I will pull out exaggeration as one specific point we might dwell on in our writing classrooms.

Gradual exaggeration can be a great technique in the funny writer's skill set, and it can empower children to edge into absurdism without them needing to have the imagination of Dali. Building up layers of exaggeration can help a mundane experience become one that is peculiar.

Procrastination Poem

Watch 'Bathroom Fiddler' for a great example of what I mean.

The poem begins normally – a kid is dawdling around in the bathroom to avoid having to go to bed. Chewing the toothbrush is how the procrastination begins, and each step is just a little more exaggerated than the previous, until we have become gradually absurd, as the young Michael stands there, dewy-eyed, 'sucking on the sponge, sucking on the sponge . . .'

As a simple writing game with the children, get them to think of a time-wasting activity, and gradually build up increasingly exaggerated and odd examples. This can be a great way to help structure the ideas of the natural surrealists too.

E.g.

I didn't want to leave Grandma's house and go home, so I asked for a boiled sweet. I unwrapped it and *pop* shoved it in my mouth.

Mmm.

I asked for another, and Dad rolled his eyes. Grandma said that's the last one, and *pop* I shoved it in my mouth.

So I asked if I could have a quick bread roll. Dad sighed and *pop* I shoved it in my mouth.

So I asked if I could have goat curry, rice and peas, and they said no, so I locked myself in the cupboard and ate cold uncooked pasta by the handful.

Exaggeration can be humorous in itself. It is something that children can recognise in their own speech and behaviour. They can see it in the actions of their classmates and siblings, and in the language of the adults in their lives.

Children can spot the funniness in conversations from home, and through just adding in a little more exaggeration, they can highlight that humour to an outsider. 'I'm Tired' is a great example of this – showing how Mum and Dad compete over who is the most exhausted.

Funny Performance

Humour is in the performance and on the page. I think the word 'performing' is far more apt than 'reading' when it comes to this kind of poetry.

Michael's YouTube performances are far more than just a man letting some words leave his mouth. Performing a funny poem engages the eyes, the eyebrows, the whole body.

It is a dance of limbs and flesh, and the words are the metronome.

Children should be able to spend as much time performing their poems as they spend writing them. This way the children can see whether the humour is working by sharing their writing with classmates.

At the basic level, this will be about taking time to make sure they are speaking clearly, enunciating enough to be understood, and are going at an appropriate pace. Building children up towards a whole-class performance is better than just expecting it of them, since this is a lot to ask of a person.

Moving from practising with one other child, to a small group and then to a larger group can be helpful. It is worth considering whether the whole-class performance is necessarily the right 'outcome' all the time too.

During lockdown, my online writing lessons showed me that some pupils can perform with a lot more flair and confidence than they would ever display in a whole group setting.

The same children who might find the live whole class performance excruciating may be much happier to perform to camera themselves, like Michael.

So then, what can we do practically to support children's comedic performances of their funny poetry?

Continue to watch poets doing their thing, and pick up their styles.

We can help the children by letting them see what they look like whilst performing. Sensitively handled – since children can be just as freaked out by their own appearance on camera as we are – this can help them to attune to what their performance looks like for others, rather than what it feels like for them.

Muting Michael

We can show a poem of Michael's on mute, as a way of emphasising how much meaning is conveyed *without* the words. Doing this can help to show them what they stand to gain by taking the time to focus on performance.

'The Hypnotiser' is great for this. Put the video on mute and play it for pupils, before they have encountered the words.

They know the title, and that's all. How much can they infer about what is happening? How many characters do they think there are? What are they doing? How are they feeling? How did Michael show this with his face and hands?

This is a good little lesson in itself, but would be great to slot into any poetry teaching sequence that will involve performance. Poetry is a full body exercise.

A final tip can be to let them perform several times. Encourage them to notice which bits of their poem 'landed', and encourage them to note this down on their draft poem. The young poets can then begin to anticipate where the audience are likely to laugh. They can focus their energies on improving that further, and on continuing to edit those parts which did not get the reaction that they had hoped for.

Several other poets who write humorously for children are great performers and readers too, and you could share their videos. I am a huge fan of AF Harrold – on YouTube you can find readings of some of his great poems like 'The Value of an Onion' and the exhaustingly irreverent 'I Want To Be A Wallaby'. For funny fiction, AL Kennedy's reading of the beginning of 'Uncle Shawn and Bill' is brilliant, and it shows a different and more relaxed approach to funny storytelling. Humza Arshad's *Little Badman* books are also brilliant, and you can see him reading it here, telling about a bee named Mustafa; the voices given to the different characters add to what is already a very funny text.

Humour and the Serious

We can explore the way in which humour and seriousness entwine. Humour can be a kind of survival language, which enables us to safely explore issues and topics that are potentially challenging or sensitive for pupils. Laura Dockrill's *My Mum's Growing Down* is a really funny poetry collection – one shortlisted for the Lollies Laugh Out Loud Book Awards in fact – and through a collection about an eccentric mother, Laura shares poems that would reassure a young reader who might feel underrepresented, as the child of a single mother.

Michael's funny poetry does not shy away from talking about childhood fears and anxieties – in fact, it is often grounded in them.

In amongst these opportunities to harness humour in our writing and performing with children, there are also responsibilities. Michael covers this well in *How To Make Children Laugh*.

We need to ensure that children's poetry does not chase the wrong kinds of laughter, and become discriminatory.

Exaggerations should not become bullying-made-art, and the jokes should always invite people in rather than push people away. The humour should encourage children to laugh together, not at the expense of each other.

At different times in society, the easiest way to get a laugh from some people has been through discriminatory jokes at the expense of the less powerful. Used effectively, humour can be a way of emboldening the voices of those who might otherwise be silenced. Almost by definition, this includes children.

Humour can be a force for good in our classrooms just as it can be a force for good in society.

4   Does It Need To Be True?

All poetry contains at least a bit of truth. Whether we are reading a detailed recount of an event, an exaggerated retelling, a subjective anecdote or even something fictional, there is something of the truth of the author in it.

If we are committed to teaching children to write and perform poetry that matters to them, then we should hope to find some authenticity in their words.

We don't need children to swear on a holy book before writing a limerick. We aren't expecting a wholly objective factual retelling of their life's happenings. Through the things that they choose to write, the details they choose to focus on and the words they select, we can find the truth of their experience.

Playing with the truth is not the same as lying. Poets can toy around with experience, by putting pen to paper.

Poetry is a game of truth. We are in charge of how much we 'let out'. We can be clearer or more obtuse. We can pour undiluted truth into the reader's breakfast bowl, or we can sprinkle bits of it into the mendacious porridge we serve them, to see whether they can still taste it.

Yes, I think poems contain some truth. Even if we think of Spike Milligan's 'On The Ning Nang Nong', one of the most popular poems amongst children . . . what possibly can be the truth of it? Well, the truth is hidden, I agree, but there's a piece of fun there. It's a kind of parody of how in these strange places, strange things happen. Insofar as it's a truth, it's just sort of saying that strange things happen in strange places. It's also truth telling in how it satirises the language.

Whole Truth or Hole Truth

Poetry can be a way of telling life stories, and Michael's writing is rife with this. Many of his poems are fragments and memories of childhood, told to entertain, whilst informing us of things that happened when he was young.

Did Michael really witness the death of the majority of his peers in a classroom with a No Breathing rule? Should we call Ofsted? Should we call for an inquiry?

No.

But does this mean Michael is a liar? He didn't tell the truth, after all. He lied to children about the existence of school prison in a popular YouTube video. Should it be taken down?

No.

The suspension of disbelief is a luxury afforded to the poet, be it

Rosen, be it you, or be it the children in your class. We can expect some truth, but we can expect some embellishment too. Spotting the difference is half of the fun.

Poems as Recounts

Michael's 'Newcomers' was a featured poem for 2019's 'National Poetry Day', which had the theme of truth. In it, Michael tells us about a 'hulky bulky thick-checked jacket that belonged to the man I would have called Grandad'.

Sometimes, you want to just tell a true story, and it doesn't require embellishment or exaggeration. The 'meaning' of the poem draws directly from the fact that it is true – it is meaningful to the writer, and it tells us something that happened.

True Recount Poem

What makes a good recount is a clear telling of the details of something that happened. What makes a good poem is the ability to make a connection with the reader or listener. Let's fuse them together.

Watch 'Newcomers' with the children. Let children discuss what it makes them think about – does it remind them of objects they or their family own?

Like in Michael's 'Newcomers' poem, let's see if we can write something that is entirely true, and tell the story with only the necessary and interesting details.

Perhaps this is something that you know is true, but others don't know it. Maybe you wanted to share a truth so that other people can know more about you.

On the poetry retreats that I run with Adisa the Verbaliser, we have plenty of time for this kind of story exchange. Some of our most meaningful and thoughtful writing comes about from group discussions back at the hostel.

Adisa had a great idea to introduce the theme of 'space', which can be interpreted in so many ways by the children. Some spoke of spacecraft, and some spoke of overcrowded homes. Some spoke of aliens, some spoke of family, and some spoke of feeling like an alien in their family.

These conversations often veered off in unexpected directions. Talk about family led to talk about growing up, and eventually, about truth and lies.

Some children took the opportunity to share small tricks and 'hacks' they use to get their own way in life, and this child's poem was a great example of this. It originated in a chat he was having with friends, and he developed it whilst we waited for the jacket potatoes to be cooked.

Lies

When I have to give homework
I get sent into a panic
I haven't done any
And school's in fifty minutes.

I always lie.
Tell them I feel sick
And as far as I know
That seems to do the trick.

But every week
I tell them I feel sick
They get sent into a panic
Not knowing the trick.

One day they took me to the doctor
I quickly told the truth
And as far as I know
That seems to do the trick.

– Jason, Year 5, Vicarage Primary, Newham

You can see how poetry can be subversive. His revelatory poem was shared with a laugh and a smile, and it led lots of other children to share the subtle techniques they've learned to avoid chores and censure.

Something about the form invites openness in much the same way as does a diary. Speaking of which . . .

One Week Poetic Diary

To attune young writers to their experiences, and to help them to see ways to translate these into poetry, try something different for a week. You can start the lesson with five minutes to write a diary entry of the day before. Encourage children to note down a daily reflection of what they did, what they felt and what they were thinking about.

Even just from these notes, children will start to see the sproutlings of truth poems about things that matter to them.

Show them 'Tricks', as an example of the kind of poem that might come about from retelling a day to day event. In Michael's case, it was the way his brother pretended to heave himself up on an invisible bar.

In addition to this, you can see from 'Tricks' and from Jason's 'Lies' poem that the theme of truth is itself a fascinating one for children to write about.

Being truthful and telling lies, concealing things that have happened and tricking others into believing things . . . all of these form part of the emotional life of all children, and it can fuel their poetry.

Poems as Advice

If recounts like those above are autobiographical, they would tend to be written in the first person. Another way in which children can tell their truths with their writing is in the form of 'advice poems', in the second person. This isn't a genre of poetry as such, but by naming it as advice, children might more easily understand the kind of writer's voice they can adopt in their writing.

Poetry can be a way for children to share experiences with each other not just through telling about them but by sharing what it has taught them. The writing classroom is not one in which the children drift around in isolation from each other. Their writing is an expression of their relationships with each other.

Again, there are plenty of Michael's poems that can be brought into the classroom to introduce this kind of writing. 'On The Move Again', by my interpretation anyway, is an emotive poem in which Michael gives his young audience some sage guidance about dealing with adversity.

Here Is My Advice

Share the video 'On The Move Again' with your class. Watch it a few times. What responses do the children have to it? Do they see it as happy or sad? Do they see it as uplifting? How could it be seen as 'advice'?

Moving from the poem, encourage the children to jot down ideas of advice they might give to others. Perhaps start with something very safe and accessible – what advice would they give to Reception children about joining their school? Take time to share thoughts, and then encourage children to branch out into more broad life advice.

What have they learned about how to be happy? How could they express this as advice to someone else?

Get them to imagine they are speaking to another child the same age as them, so that they don't default to seeing us – the teachers – as the audience.

Poems as Reflection

Writing can be a kind of thinking. We know this intuitively as adults, but we don't attend to this kind of writing much in school. Spontaneous jottings don't need a planning grid or a plot mountain.

Through a poem, a writer can sometimes combine 'reporting' and 'reflecting'. For our children, this might be a way for them to share about events in their lives, or significant conversations they've had. In putting together the memory with their reflection on it, children can be encouraged to process life's happenings.

This is something that they probably haven't done before. It can help us appreciate the good times and reflect on challenging times.

We don't just write what we think about, we sometimes think what we write about.

For this reason, it is worth exercising caution and not opening a space for conversations that we aren't willing to make time for. The trade-off for encouraging real expression in the classroom is that we become more fully human in our interactions, and this carries a greater ethical responsibility than if we are getting the children to complete a gap fill haiku about something we are all equally bored by.

Reflection Poem

'Going Through The Old Photos' is a good example of this kind of writing. Watch it. The poem tells us of the time Michael discovered that he had had an older brother named Alan who died in infancy, after having seen an old photo of his Mum with a baby on her knee.

This activity should begin with a reminder that we all have a right to privacy, and that nobody should feel obliged to share or write about anything they don't want to. It may be better framed as writing about positive or funny memories.

Talk about how in our life some moments might seem more important or significant than others. Have you ever had a conversation that felt very special, or that has stuck in your head? Have you had moments that seem like they have changed your life?

Perhaps we can take time to jot some things down in a private notepad. Then we can open up a space to share in small groups, if we want to do so.

Show Michael's poem, 'Going Through The Old Photos'. Watching together, describe Michael's discovery of the old photo as a significant moment, just like they had been talking about their own.

Tell children that the poem had a structure in which
1) the memory and conversation was retold
2) the poet shared how he felt about the memory at the time
3) the poet shared what he feels about it now.

Give time for children to familiarise themselves with this basic organising structure and let them develop their poem in a similar way, starting with a retelling and moving on to their emotional response to it.

It is worth reiterating that this kind of writing is likely to elicit an emotional response. It should do.

True or False?

The examples so far have been pretty truthful. They have encouraged children to find ways to share true stories and to express their true feelings in a more or less literal way.

Other forms of poetry writing can be explained as exaggerated truths. They can embellish for effect. These embellishments might make it more funny, if that is what they want to do. They might slightly hide the truth, and open up a little bit of ambiguity. Or they might derail the truth into lies. True or false? Who can say?

In my experience of running poetry retreats with children, I have seen something fascinating. Children's poems are often more truthful when they are invited to exaggerate, or hide some fantasy or untruths within them. The permission to be ambiguous can be the safety net, above which children feel confident to tackle the high wire of truth-telling.

'Pretty Much True' Poem

This activity will get children to write about something true, but embellish it through exaggeration. It isn't about diving off into pure fantasy, but just leaning on lies to make the poetic tale a bit more entertaining or funny.

Start a conversation with the children about the best and worst things they have ever tasted? Did they taste the bad stuff on purpose or accidentally?

Let them know that Michael has a great poem about this. Play 'Orange Juice' and watch it with them. (This is a great example of whole-body poetry performance too.)

Let the children know that the story is 'Pretty Much True'. And even the bits that are not entirely true, are just exaggerations of the truth. Do we think he really danced around the house for an hour to get rid of the taste? No! It's an exaggeration!

On to the writing, get the children to write a true story about how they, or someone they know, came to eat something that was disgusting. Keep it mostly true, but when it gets to describing the taste, encourage them to experiment with exaggeration. How bad was the taste? What was the reaction? Did their lips fall off? Did they weep to their nana? Did they drink a litre of yoghurt to get the taste away?

Encourage children to share the poems with each other, as small performances. Expect laughter as a marker of a good bit of exaggeration!

With 'Orange Juice' it is fairly easy for us to guess which bits are true and which bits are false. It is very believable that someone pinched the juice and it is believable that Michael may have had a cunning plan to get revenge. It is not believable that someone's mouth is on fire.

Another playful truth game is True or False.

Because so many of Michael's poems are grounded in autobiography, and because we know his errant sense of humour, and because he is revered, he is very well placed to dupe us with cheeky falsehoods.

The 'True or False' videos on the channel are a great showcase of this.

Without any of the facial expressions that would suggest he is tricking us, Michael tells anecdotal tales of unusual things that have happened.

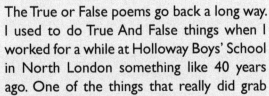

The True or False poems go back a long way. I used to do True And False things when I worked for a while at Holloway Boys' School in North London something like 40 years ago. One of the things that really did grab some of those Year 7s and Year 8s and even Year 9 was to tell them true weird stories alongside weird untrue stories, and to set them the task of working out which one is true. The true one involved me being knocked down in the road, and not remembering anything.

It's always stuck in the back of my mind that it's an interesting area to get to because it's actually about the texture of writing. Whether you can conceal untruths behind a true surface. This is what Daniel Defoe does in *Journal Of The Plague Year* and *Moll Flanders*. To a certain extent, Swift does with *Gulliver's Travels*. This is an 18th century thing as well, because they couldn't believe that people believed the stuff that they made up. Somebody once reacted to *Gulliver's Travels* by saying 'I didn't believe half of it'. Well what about the other half?!

The most I've pushed it in my own poems is on the one about the rats on New Cross Gate station. It started off as a truth. I was watching rats on New Cross Gate station and then I sort of married it up to the Pied Piper. Anyway I'm giving away secrets here, I really shouldn't ... It was absolutely true! A man came along and ate a rat, yeah. Absolutely true.

Rats is one of my favourite videos on the channel. Michael tells us about the conversation he had waiting for the late night train from New Cross Gate, when he and some other commuters spotted some rats. He gives some specific details, such as that he had bought a hummus wrap from the Beirut Canteen, and this adds to the authenticity of his tale. But then other details in the story are pretty barbaric, such as when the man beside him speared one of the rats on a toasting fork.

True or False Poems

Ask the children whether it is easy to tell if someone is telling the truth? How certain can you be? Can someone start with a lie and hide the truth in it? Can they start with the truth and hide lies in it?

Share 'Rats' with them.

What do they make of it? Is it true or false? Get them to watch it again, noticing that Michael gives some specific details and doesn't seem surprised or horrified when the man begins toasting the rat.

I wonder if they can come up with a story like this, told in the form of an anecdotal poem. Make it a mix of true and false, and see if you can tell it in a way that makes it hard for people to tell the difference.

If they want a prompt, you could begin with "I saw something a bit odd last weekend . . . "

There are other True or False poems on the channel, including 'A Whale Got On My Bus', 'Cows' and 'Cucumber'.

5   Does It Have To Make Sense?

It can be a challenge for children to recognise what nonsense is. Raised in a sharp-edged world of right and wrong, nonsense hovers playfully between the poles. Nonsense poetry doesn't make sense in a literal way, but it isn't completely 'senseless' either. For children to enjoy and embrace nonsense poetry, we need for them to get comfortable with ambiguity.

Whilst our minds might leap immediately to the limericks of Edward Lear or the mimsy borogoves of Lewis Carroll, nonsense poetry has a longer and more global tradition, such as in the writings of Sukumar Ray from India, Daniil Kharms from Russia, and in the traditional tales of Mulla Nasruddin, found across the Middle East.

Pumpkin Grumpkin: Nonsense Tales from around the World, edited by John Agard and Grace Nichols, is a great starting point to broaden our nonsense repertoire.

What binds a lot of nonsense literature together is a playfulness with language. It often detaches the meanings from the words, and waggles them about a little. Writing nonsense poetry is like a surreal game, in which wisdom, wordplay, confusion and bemusement all lather up and wrestle each other.

This is the point that is perhaps trickier for children to grasp as writers: writing nonsense requires a good understanding of what does make sense.

The nonsense poet Anushka Ravishankar writes 'I studied mathematics, so I have a special affinity for logic, and by extension, illogical nonsense'. Our teaching should help children to see the method behind the madness, and to appreciate that even on a flight of fancy, there is often a skilled pilot.

I really like Sampurna Chattarji's personal definition of nonsense, and I think it is a good starting point for our own work here.

> 'To me, nonsense is a game we play in which humour and insight, imagination and anarchy bounce in amazing (and amazingly rigorous) patterns on the trampoline of language.'

Let's get jumping.

How might children write nonsense?

Given the freedom to write nonsense, children will often write things that are senseless. The difference is the lack of meaning, or the absence perhaps of any structure. It's sometimes tough to know what is and is not working with nonsense. The child-writer may have something very clear in mind. When they talk about their writing, it can make a lot more sense in context.

When teaching children to write nonsense poetry, we can focus on the use of 'nonsense words', the role of grammar, surreal ideas and the playfulness of contradiction and impossibility. Here is a poem one of the students created on our Poetry Retreat.

The Fork

The fork climbed up the tree, to find his missing shoe:
"Aargh!" the tree screamed, and didn't know what to do.

The plate climbed up the tree, to find his missing fork who was looking for his missing shoe:
"Aargh!" the tree screamed, and didn't know what to do

The table climbed up the tree to find his missing plate who was looking for his missing fork who was looking for his missing shoe:
"Aaargh! the tree screamed, and didn't know what to do.

The sofa climbed up the tree to find his missing table who was looking for his missing plate who was looking for his missing fork who was looking for his missing shoe:

But this time the tree did not scream but instead he shook all the objects out of his leaves, to the ground:

"Aargh!" all the objects screamed, and didn't know what to do.

– Asi, Keir Hardie Primary, Newham

It has a narrative structure to it, and one that is playfully repetitive and farcical. I love that she referred to the fork, plate, table and sofa as 'objects' again at the end, despite them being her main actors. I especially love that she chose to make them scream in confusion even after having been referred to as objects. It reminds me of Michael's poems 'Fast Food' and 'Little Rabbit Foo Foo'.

Asi managed to create nonsense by telling a weird and contradictory story which makes grammatical sense but no literal sense.

Here are four ways we can introduce nonsense poetry writing with our pupils.

Help!

Michael's poem 'Help', found 44 seconds into his 'Nonsense' video, can be used as a stepping-stone into rhyming nonsense. Watch it with the children.

The poem uses rhyming pairs, like 'There's a clock in my sock, there's an egg on my leg'. Perhaps your children will get the idea just by listening to it, or perhaps they could begin by writing down as many body parts as possible. They could then come up with as many words that rhyme with the body parts as possible, and think about which would be the strangest pairing.

Let's say I chose the body part 'hip'. If my list of rhyming words included 'chip', 'zip', 'lip', 'rip', 'grip', 'ship', 'flip' and 'warship', I would need to think about what would be the most suitable choice.

I might favour one syllable for flow, so 'warship' is out. It would need to be a noun – so 'grip' and 'flip' would probably be out. It would need to be something weird that I could still imagine. 'Ship' doesn't quite work because the scale is off – I can't imagine a ship on a hip. For me, I think 'zip' or even 'lip' would be the best choice.

This is my personal choice though, and the children would make their own. Going through the thought process is part of the exercise. Choosing the best rhyming words can be what tips the balance between 'no sense' and 'sense'.

Perhaps you can borrow Michael's "Help help! Nothing's right! I can't find my ears and my pants are too tight!" to start the poem. Each child could illustrate their strangest line.

The Logic of Nonsense

We will focus on nonsensical interaction, using Michael's video 'Logic'. This very short poem draws upon wordplay and jokes, and we can use it to get children to toy about with cause and effect when they are telling peculiar tales.

Watch 'Logic'. Ask the children what they think – do they find it funny? Does it make them think? What does it make them think? You'll probably get a mixed range of responses – it is very different from most of Michael's other videos.

Focus in on Michael's second part, about Jack. Could we create something similar? Get them sharing about different things they are grateful for about their lives, in a tongue-in-cheek way. As an example, you could say something like "I'm so pleased I've got a dog . . . because we've got so many dog toys at home" or "I'm so pleased I'm not Norwegian . . . because I can only speak English."

Play around as a class coming up with ideas that work. We are looking for children to see that these examples confuse the consequence with the thing that caused it.

Why do I have dog toys? Because I have a dog. Why do I speak English, because I was raised in England, not Norway. This activity gets children to play around with the logic of cause and effect.

The Grammar of Nonsense

Share Lewis Carroll's 'The Jabberwocky' with pupils. Texts are accessible online, and you can share Michael's reading. There are an abundance of things you can do to immerse children in this poem – they can act out elements of it, embody what they think certain words like 'wiffling' and 'gallumphing' mean and can do great things with illustration. This latter idea will help to show that the ambiguity of Carroll's nonsense words is what makes it so powerful – different people picture different scenes, inspired by different interpretations of his nonsense words.

For our writerly purposes, we want children to understand why it still seems to make sense as a story, despite the invented words. Then, they can experiment in similar ways.

Watch the poem several times, considering why it is that we interpret certain words as adjectives and some as verbs, based on the position in the sentence, and their suffixes. With other words, we can infer meaning from the nonsense words based on what they sound like – 'frabjous' suggests (to me anyway) frankly fabulous and joyous. 'Frumious' suggests dubious and furious.

Encourage the children to work together to write their own scenes hunting a creature, to practise the skill of grammatically-accurate but semantically peculiar nonsense.

Impossible and Contradictory Nonsense

Contradiction is a feature of lots of nonsense poetry. This could be about impossible events, like the rapid growing and shrinking of Alice, after diving in the rabbit hole. But it can also be created through dissonance, stating that two contradictory things are true.

Michael's 'True or False' poems are good examples of impossible events. Watch 'Dentist', and hear Michael's earnestly-told tale about when the dentist implanted a clock onto his tooth. Perhaps watching a few of the True of False videos, such as 'Rats' and 'A Whale Got On My Bus' would be helpful here to make the point that in nonsense, part of the fun is about telling something very untrue as if it were very true.

To explore dissonance, which often comes out in the grammar of nonsense poetry, begin by sharing the famous poem – anonymous and widely available online – 'One Fine Day In The Middle of the Night'.

Which pairs of opposites can children find in the poem? What does it make them imagine? Is it possible to imagine contradictory things, such as dead men standing up to fight, and being back-to-back facing each other.

Encourage the children to work in groups to collate as many pairs of opposites as possible in a limited amount of time. An opposites challenge. Then, encourage them to use these pairs as peculiar source material to create their own contradictory nonsense.

6   Can It Be About My Life?

I want to be clear about this one. Yes.

When children in schools encounter poetry mostly through reading comprehension tasks, even if they go on to then write poetry in response to it, we end up with the same problem: the poetry they engage with is exclusively about the lives of others.

When we add to this the fact that the poetry for children that teachers know about tends to be predominantly a white, straight, middle-class male collection, a gap develops between the poetry our students encounter and the lives that they lead.

There are several things that can be done in response to this, and many things are happening already. We can diversify the range of poets whose work we share beyond the narrow range we likely encountered in our own schooling. These poets do exist, but many do not get the same exposure, familiarity and name-recognition.

Another idea could be to seek out themed anthologies on topics that children can connect with. AF Harrold's *Midnight Feasts* collection of food poems features brilliant contributions from a diverse range of established and newer poets whose work is found less often in classrooms, such as Imtiaz Dharker, Ian McMillan, Chitra Soundar and Kat Francois.

But beyond this, the most powerful way in which we can alter children's perceptions of poetry is through writing rather than reading.

We need to show children that their lives, experiences, anecdotes, thoughts, loves, fears, desires and anxieties are all worthy of being written about poetically.

Poetry can be about their lives, and by encouraging them to write from their experience – whether literally or swaddled in metaphor – we can democratise poetry.

Poetry belongs to our students, just as much as it does to anybody else.

The Ethics Of A Writing Classroom

In *Did I Hear You Write?*, Michael suggests that all children come to school with a breadth of experience, which he terms their culture. 'The problem is that unless we ask them questions about this culture, we never find out that it exists.'

Children's social and personal cultures encapsulate much of what they 'tell' about themselves, and how they see their changing place in the world. A list of elements of the culture of children is included as an Appendix, but some examples include sayings, jokes, pride, regret, embarrassment, food, dreams, nightmares and fears.

Each of these topics has the potential to invite children's own experiences onto the page.

This does not require us to remove all structure, direction and form from our writing classrooms. It is not a case of 'over to you, guys . . . spill your secrets'. If we did it in this way, pupils will likely feel uncertain and cast adrift, rather than newly liberated.

Authentic writing can grow from authentic conversation.

In preparation for our writing about funny moments, for example, the best thing we can do as a kind of 'planning' is to open up an exchange of free-flowing stories and anecdotes. This requires a kind of attentive listening that is sometimes challenging for children and adults alike. Too often, what we call listening is really just 'waiting to speak', and the fast pace and pressure of the classroom can feed this.

Children are anxious not to say something wrong, so they focus all their thinking on their own responses rather than listening.

In a classroom, we know that some children will have ideas ready to share immediately, but for those students who prefer to let things percolate more, they can benefit from hearing others before sharing their own thoughts. And then, perhaps, those immediate speakers can think anew on their own instinctive responses, having heard the contributions of their more circumspect pals.

This requires an ethical commitment from us as teachers. If we cannot hold ourselves to these standards, then encouraging children to write authentic and meaningful things about their lives would be unfair and irresponsible. Here are three elements of that commitment.

1. All writers should be able to share their writing only if/ when they feel comfortable doing so. This requires trust on our part. Their writing belongs to them, not to us.
2. We need to facilitate a culture of respectful listening, where there is no ridicule. Children need to be able to put their faith in the group if they are going to write openly.
3. We need to share clear expectations, and hold ourselves to them. Applying parameters to the writing does not need to limit children's self-expression.

When I lead a poetry retreat, I make it clear at the beginning that the only steadfast expectation is that each of us – adults and children alike – will have two pages in the anthology, so will submit some poetry at the end of the week.

Some may choose to broadcast every idea, anecdote, edit and completed poem to the group. They may want feedback, recognition, assurance, praise, or attention – each is valid. Other children may select just one adult or one other child with whom they want to share their progress and ideas. Some spend time listening before they feel safe enough to share, and once they do so, they do so regularly.

This diversity of responses is probably a sign that the writing culture you are creating is working – authentic writing can only come from authentic writers, and real writers don't follow the same approach as each other.

For a child to share their meaningful writing with us is one of the greatest privileges we get as a teacher. It is like being welcomed to browse their personal diaries. It is a whisper in our ear. It is an invitation to peer into their mind.

The activities in this section are a little different to in other chapters. The point I made earlier was that we don't want children to always have to write in response to or in the style of a particular poem that they have been picking away at in reading lessons.

The videos on Michael's channel which are featured in these activities are chosen because they can enrich the discussions at the beginning of the writing session. Michael's storytelling and anecdotes can sit aside your own, in your classrooms.

Delicious Conversation

This activity uses food as an example topic, but could work with any of the different themes and topics that are listed in the Appendix.

We are sharing the idea that when we talk about food, we often end up talking about so much more. Food stories lead us to think about things like growing up, and culture, and family, for example.

Talk about which foods you associate with particular family members you grew up with. Perhaps fresh tomatoes take you back to your grandad's greenhouse. Perhaps the smell of chicken biryani reminds you of attending a cousin's wedding. Share some of your own stories and invite children to do so. Give time to this – it may be slow to start, but typically once children begin sharing, their classmates find it easier to do so.

Encourage children to note down some ideas about foods that they associate with different family members into their writing books. This will give children the chance to start recording the seeds of their poetry, for those who are ready.

Bring it back to a whole group conversation – food can bring up a range of emotions in our memory. Food can be associated with happy times and fun times, but can also be associated with sadness and stress. Ask a few questions around this – can any of you remember having to eat something you really didn't like? Which foods always make you happy? What happens when you are eating them?

Again, these questions and children's responses are all about encouraging a deepening of the talk, so that children go beyond 'I like crisps' into more specific memories and anecdotes relating to food.

At this point, tell the children that lots of poets write about food, and they tell us about more than just food.

Share Michael's poem 'Fried Egg'.

After giving the children a chance to watch it, make the point that Michael's poem wasn't just about 'fried eggs' in general, or whether or not he liked them. It was about a specific day when he and his brother bickered about how best to clean up the yolk from a leaky egg.

Poetry captures specific moments. Get the children to think of specific food memory moments and record them into their notepads. Perhaps they too have invented challenges and games with siblings? Perhaps they want to develop more specific details about the food memories they have already listed.

Share a few more food poems. From the channel, these could include 'Bagel', 'Corned Beef' or 'I Don't Like Custard'. If you have poetry books and anthologies, children can read some food poems aloud. The best I know of is 'Midnight Feasts'.

Encourage children to share their own anecdotes together, but without any unnecessary details. What is the heart of their food stories?

Encourage them to write them down, in free verse.

Give children time to share their readings with each other, encouraging them to edit to emphasise the areas that their audience find most interesting.

Finally, open up a space for any children who wish to do so to share their poems, whether work-in-progress or complete. Encourage children to share their responses to each other's experiences, as well as to the poem itself.

This structure can work for all of the themes listed in the Appendix. Experiment, and see which topics lead to the richest conversations with your pupils.

Anecdote to Camera

This activity looks more explicitly at the performative aspect of poetry as storytelling. Children will get the chance to focus on a specific detail of an anecdote, and tell it 'confessionally' to the camera, in the style that Michael performs his videos on the channel.

Share with the children that in this activity, we won't be writing long poems, but instead we will be focusing on how we can tell snippets of interesting details in a way that makes them memorable.

Watch 'The Youngest'

Tell the children that we are going to come up with some 'snippets' ourselves, about the most annoying thing about being 'the oldest', 'the youngest', 'the middle child' or 'the only child'; perhaps this could also look at the specific details of being 'step-child' or 'foster child' or 'adopted child' for children for whom that applies and who would want a space to talk about it.

Share that we will watch the video again, but be thinking about two questions. What did Michael find most annoying about being the youngest? What conversations did he share with us, to tell us about it?

Watch 'The Youngest' again.

Encourage children to pair up and talk about their perspectives on the most annoying thing about being youngest/oldest/middle/only/step/foster/adopted child. Encourage them to notice what makes them and each other laugh – these are the bits we need to keep and focus on.

Share that today we are going to not spend too much time editing and crafting – we want to capture a 30 second snippet of response from them. We will be recording a video, like Michael does for the YouTube channel.

Notice what he does with his face, hands and voice to tell the story. Watch one more time, then give children the chance to practise and to record each other.

Make time to watch these back – the opportunity to see themselves on camera is different to performing to each other, and can lead to interesting reflection and self-observation.

7   Do I Need To Write Properly?

I think there's plenty of opportunity for children to discover that almost everything that comes out of our mouths can be put onto the page and you can transliterate it. Even noises. So you know – boing and crararaannng – you can experiment with noises and put them down. So everything from the cadences of our speech, the slangs we use, can go onto the page. Obviously the conventions we use in classrooms are important, about obscenities and hurting people verbally, so I'm not saying anything goes.

After all, dramatists and screenwriters do this all the time, so why can't school children? It's a high art form, isn't it. So, you know, there's plenty of scope for these things and we don't have to say 'Oh, but it's not proper'. Take Shakespeare, take film scripts. What do they do? Some of the greatest art films have got people grunting at each other, and muttering and talking in slang. Well somebody wrote that down.

And so I think there's a great scope for children experimenting with that, and poetry is one way you can do it. As it happens, scripts and sketches and plays are another

> way to do it as well, but the advantage of poems is that you can put them into extended monologues, so you can sort of speak a monologue. You can speak a set of thoughts. You can speak a dream, and you can put dialogue in it or it can be just your spoken voice.

Poetry is political because language is political. When we look at creative writing in a school setting, the question of 'correct English' soon comes up. Through the imperatives of the National Curriculum, certain elements of the teaching of English have been elevated beyond their station.

To be against the SPAG tests does not mean that you are against the teaching of grammar. I love grammar teaching, and all the fascination that can be sparked in children's minds when they recognise the peculiar scaffolds through which we structure our words and build meaning. Within our grammar rules, we find the masonry for the world's languages; the conventions and etymologies that sit beneath our sentences and words all tell the centuries-old tale of human culture.

But that's certainly not the vibe I get when asking a child to tick which out of four statements contains a correctly-used semi-colon. Tickbox grammar tests are used as a more measurable and quantifiable proxy for a much more challenging thing to measure; a child's ability to write.

Beneath a pretended neutrality, there is an underlying assumption that there is only one correct way to use the English Language.

Our response in our classrooms is not that there are no rules whatsoever, but that there are different correct uses of language, and that not all are equally valued in society. Language is ever-changing, always growing and pulsing to the rhythms of society and culture. It resists categorisation.

Poetry gives us the opportunity to broaden children's understanding of the versatile potential of language, but in schools we can sometimes do the opposite. We end up taking poems that are enigmatic, complex and beautiful, and pinning false absolutes to them.

'I didn't ask you to question what it means to be human, Year 6, just please underline the adverbs in it.'

If we were to insist that poetry always needs to use 'proper words' and adhere to particular structures, we narrow their expectation and appreciation of both poetry and of language itself.

We should aim to get children writing authentically about things that matter, and they should be able to express this in ways that are real.

This may include so-called 'non-standard English', slang, multilingual blending, dialectal and colloquial terms, and a suspension of prosaic grammar and punctuation rules. This could mean, for some children, that finally the voice in their head can come out onto the page, in the knowledge that it will be accepted.

Slang

The main distinctions between 'slang' and 'accepted English' are power and time. One generation's slang may become the next generation's common parlance. It is through slang that many words with foreign origin find their ways to English. Slang grows organically from culture's need for new words to capture new experiences, new feelings, new situations and new phenomena.

In our poetry lessons, when we want children to write authentically, and express what is meaningful to them, we need to sometimes erode the distinction between slang and 'not slang'. Let words be words.

Definitions Poem

Explain that the children will know lots of words that adults probably don't understand. Can they think of any?

Prompt them to think about the stuff that they talk about with friends. At the time of writing, this might well be YouTube, memes and gaming for our older primary pupils. Each of these generates lots of language. It may also open up sharing of dialectal or cultural words.

Most of the students I have taught are from Muslim families, so many of the words they shared with me in this activity included words related to their faith – the maulana who teaches at their mosque, or how much they want to become a hafiz by studying Hifz, and memorising the Qu'ran. But alongside this, there was plenty of East London slang mixed in with internet culture.

Encourage children to contribute to a huge class list. Be playful and celebrate your ignorance. This can work particularly well if you teach in a place that you yourself were not raised. Let them be your dialectal tour guides.

Once a huge list has been collated, encourage children to write a 'letter poem' to you, short and brief, explaining a word and giving you sage advice on how to use it, and how not to.

This one was shared with me from a cold-hearted Year 5 pupil.

Dear Sir
We need to talk about 'bare jokes'.
It's not jokes about bears.
It means 'so funny'
Your bear jokes are cringe
They're not bare jokes.

Less explicitly about definitions, we can simply encourage children to write with the language they use when they speak. This isn't about 'preserving' slang, like in an exhibition, but just letting it into our writing. Sharing some of Michael's videos where he mixes the Yiddish terms in with English can support children to get the idea here.

Rather than Michael writing about Yiddish terms, he is just talking about childhood, which – for him – happened to include lots of it.

Examples here could include 'Bubbe and Zeyde'.

Multilingualism

Many children we teach speak more than one language, and very few of them get the chance to use and celebrate this aptitude in school, unless they are bilingual in European languages. This is a grave injustice.

Encouraging children to weave their languages together, if they would like to do so, can have a lot of benefits. It allows many children to write in a way that is more akin to the way they use language in talk; for example, using English with their friends at school, then switching to Sylheti with their grandparents at home time. They might use a mixture when talking with siblings.

Encouraging children to blend their languages in poetry also opens up the possibility of using words from other languages that don't necessarily translate directly.

Watch 'Bubbe and Zeyde' – why does it make sense for Michael to refer to them this way in the poem? Simple. That is what he called them. Similarly, children may find it interesting to see how they feel differently about their writing when they select the words that they actually use. Most of my students refer to their mums as 'ma' but it is not a word we ever use in school.

Family Talk

To encourage children to write in the style of the spoken word, a good writing activity is for children to relay family conversations. This could be an imagined conversation that captures the way people typically talk, or children may enjoy the chance to spy on the conversations, and make jottings of things that are actually said.

Many of Michael's videos would work well for this, especially those talking about misadventures with his siblings. Share 'I'm Just Going Out' with the children, and ask them whether it reminds them of any conversations that happen in their house.

Next share 'Washing Up'. Again, ask children if it made them think of anything from home – what sort of arguments do they get into with brothers and sisters?

This time, encourage the children to write a version of this poem that is framed around the conversation they have. Focus on Michael's brother saying 'Hard cheeeeese!'. What do the children's siblings say that annoys them? Focus on

Michael shouting 'Oh horrible!' and 'Oy!! That got me in the face!". What sort of things do the children shout when they are annoyed? Include these in the poem.

A great way to motivate older primary school writers could be to encourage their use of dialectal and colloquial terms. The challenge is that for many children, especially younger ones, their language just 'is', and they won't be able to separate what is local language from what is 'national' English.

As a kid, I didn't know that mardy was a South Yorkshire term – I just saw it as a word to describe someone who was having a tantrum.

For an adult writer, the local words of our youth can stir up rich pangs of nostalgia – for children, it is a further way of encouraging them to write things that are significant and meaningful in their own voices.

As an activity, ask them to speak to family about words that people only really say in their local area, and to bring them in to share.

The unifying thread across these activities is the recognition that there are many valid uses of the English language. In making space for the breadth of children's spoken language – which may be rich in slang, dialect and multilingual blending – we are making a political point too.

We are helping them to recognise that a hierarchy of value exists in society, which elevates the status of some people's English language above others.

Whether we are teaching the children whose language benefits from this unfairness, or those whose language is denigrated, we should resist it.

Given explicit permission and encouragement to do so, many children can and will write evocatively in a way that draws their languages together on the page, building up the meaningfulness of it all. The fact that they might seek permission to do so, rather than just doing it, is quite telling.

There is not one correct English towards which our young writers must adapt and conform.

8 How Do We Teach Poetic Structures Creatively?

There is a misconception that structure and creativity are in some way opposed. It can be imagined that being creative means doing everything from scratch. Structure can be seen as limiting or curtailing the creativity of a writer.

I don't think this is the case, and your kids probably don't either.

What this section is all about is how we can balance freedom and constraint in order to show children a different route to creative self-expression. We'll explore different poetic forms like sonnets and limericks, we will also look at the massive potential for music to transform and energise our poetry classrooms.

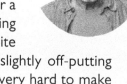

I'd say it can take more creativity to write within a structure, than without one. If you have a form, like a limerick or a sonnet or a cinquain or any of these, then it's interesting because you have to work around for quite a long time to make things work. The slightly off-putting thing for young children is that it is very very hard to make it work.

It can be wildly frustrating when you can't fit into the shape you are using. I don't actually weep but I do sometimes shake my hand about in frustration. It is an interesting form of creativity to work within the shapes and forms that the history of poetry and rap and so on have given us.

Borrowing Poem Shapes

In *What is Poetry? The Essential Guide to Reading and Writing Poems* Michael referred to sonnets, limericks and ballads as 'poem shapes' that can be borrowed. I love this way of thinking about forms. It demystifies them without undermining them. Children know that a shape is something that they can play with and build things from.

There are so many 'poem shapes' we can choose from – I'm focusing on sonnets and limericks because they are forms we are all likely to know something about, and may already have them nestled within our English curriculum.

The message I'm wanting to get across here is applicable across all 'form' poems, as opposed to free verse: we should introduce forms playfully. We should note the challenges of sticking to it, and still provide space for children to write from their experience.

It is a lot easier for children (and adults) to understand how these forms work *as a reader* than it is to do so *as a writer*. It is a lot easier to recognise the features of a sonnet than to write one effectively for ourselves.

The same is true of many of these forms; they may appear deceptively simple when considered just as a list of their features, but are more challenging when we put them all together.

It is a desirable challenge.

We don't want to destroy the children's confidence by saying "Now you know what one is, go and write a sonnet guys!".

We should not pretend that it is that simple.

Writing Sonnets

Let's look first at sonnets. There are different forms of sonnet, with different rhyme schemes. The rhyme pattern in a Spenserian sonnet has an ABAB BCBC CDCD EE structure for example. We will look more at the Shakespearean style here. The Shakespearean sonnet has an ABAB CDCD EFEF GG rhyme pattern. The fourteen lines are split into three quatrains (four line verses) and a rhyming couplet. They are written in iambic pentameter. Themes are typically of love and romance.

If we spent a bit of time explaining the meaning of these terms, the children would have no difficulty in spotting these features.

As is the mantra of this book, we should encourage children to write about what they like. Sonnet writing is hard enough without asking them to also invent an emotional world they don't inhabit, or to step into the psyche of another character.

If we are teaching sonnets to introduce children to the form, then we can ease them into this by relaxing the need for a theme of romance and love. Turning the writing of a sonnet into 'playing with a poem shape', we can get children focusing on the rhyme scheme, the meter and the fourteen line structure.

Mundane Sonnets

Writing sonnets about boring everyday stuff is fun. It can enable children to focus on the structure, by drawing on aspects of life they know so well. Funnily enough, it can also create some technically-accomplished and whimsical sonnets.

Spend time talking about the word 'mundane'. Sometimes, people think poetry is only for special moments – to commemorate battles, or emotional moments, or significant times. What if we were to see things differently, and use the shape of a sonnet to tell anecdotes?

Share anecdotes together about mundane moments – exactly how they get ready for school in the morning, what does a typical Sunday look like and so on.

Have a model ready of your own creation, which demonstrates the devices, but then – once you have explored this model with them – take the time to write a new one alongside them too.

Joining in as a writer with them will enable you to share in the challenges that they will likely encounter. They will perhaps neglect meaning out of a desire to rhyme. They will perhaps lack rhyme out of a desire to tell the anecdote. Share the struggle with them.

A girl in my Year 5 class wrote a lilting sonnet about how disgusting the London Underground is.

One boy surprised me with a love poem he addressed to the most handsome boy in the class. It ends:

He is so incredibly handsome
His eyes are really amazing
To save him I'd pay any ransom
When I see his eyes I can't stop gazing

I have to reveal he is a cute elf
I admit I have a crush on myself

Limericks

Limericks can be covered in a similar way, and are a better option for younger pupils. The structure of a limerick is that it has five lines and an AABBA rhyme scheme. The lines are made up of trios of syllables, called anapests. The beat of an anapest is unstressed-unstressed-stressed.

It is da-da-DUM.

The first, second and fifth lines have three anapests, and the third and fourth have two. The lines all start on the second beat of the anapest.

So a limerick is like this. Notice how the syllables don't need to be exact so long as the beat is. The 'er' in Doncaster sits after the DUM, but before the next line.

da-DUM da-da-DUM da-da-DUM
da-DUM da-da-DUM da-da-DUM
da-DUM da-da-DUM
da-DUM da-da-DUM
da-DUM da-da-DUM da-da-DUM

There ONCE was a MAN from DonCAST(er)
Who IGnored a WEAther foreCAST(er)

(He) said MATE don't be BAR(my)
There'll BE(no) tsuNA(mi)
And THIS caused a NATional disAST(er)

The fact that limericks are so firmly associated with Edward Lear and nonsense poetry is perhaps helpful for us in the classroom. We can focus on supporting and encouraging the children to play with language in order to master rhyme and rhythm. If their limericks tiptoe into nonsense, then so be it – it's the perfect time for it.

Let's Play with Limericks

Explain that today we are going to be playing with limericks. Before we make our own, we need to see how they work. Bring up exhibit A, which is a sequence of six limericks from the 'Michael Rosen Nonsense' video (from 5 mins 40).

Watch all six and then focus on one.

> There was an old man from Crewe
> Who wanted to know how to moo
> He studied a cow
> To try to learn how
> But all he could do was boo

Unpick it with the children – what are the features of this poem? Ensure that before we move on to writing, the children are aware of the structure, beat and rhyme pattern.

Let them borrow from Michael's structure, perhaps coming up with a list of place names in the first instance. Instead of Crewe, where could the person be from? Use this to show the importance of a place name that can be rhymed with. Bury works better than Liverpool. Bristol works better than Southminster.

This early talk – trying out place names to see which rhyming words they can think of – is what will ultimately determine whether the limerick 'works' as a limerick.

Freedom and Constraint

What we are doing by introducing the poem shapes in this way is showing children that they can be creative within a structure. Perhaps in school, children get used to the idea that having a 'scaffold' means they are not doing well. They see it as an aid for the strugglers. Perhaps they sometimes get rewarded with 'free writing' or 'free choice'.

Let's not do this.

In the way that we talk about forms like sonnets and limericks, and other 'poem shapes', children can come to recognise that writing expressively within a structure is creative.

Music and Rhythm

Even when poems don't fit the more formally defined categories of poem shapes, there will often be a structure that holds it together.

Rhythm.

If you spend time exploring Michael's videos, you will see that lots of them are narrative and anecdotal, and there are lots of kinds of poems. Some rhyme and some don't, but generally speaking, most of them contain a beat.

At the most explicit end of the musicality scale, there are songs. Enjoy sharing the riotously peculiar 'Bugs Go Wild', 'Watermelon' and 'Susanna's A Funiful Cow', for example – the songs are accompanied by music, as well as animated fruit.

But you will also find lots of musicality and rhythm in many of Michael's other poems.

The Michael Rosen Rap

This activity gives children a chance to announce themselves to the world.

Share 'The Michael Rosen Rap'.

Before you do anything else with it, watch again but ask the children to clap along with it.

After the second watch, ask them how they knew when to clap. Talk about how the length of the lines and Michael's rhythm made it clear that there was a beat.

Get the children to chant

'A Hip, Hop, A Hip Hop Hap – I'm Giving You All The Michael Rosen Rap'

Make sure they pause after 'All' – talk about how this pause means we say 'The Michael Rosen Rap' quicker.

Encourage the children to write their own versions, using their name and the stems that Michael uses.

When I was 1, When I was 2 . . . and so on.

Children won't need lots of explicit teaching about this – the rhythm of poetry is what appeals to so many of them in the first place. The best example to explore here – as a written poem but also as a performance – is the classic.

We're Going On A Bear Hunt

This poem is rich in pretty much all aspects of children's poetry – we have melody, we have repetition, we have onomatopoeia and there are so many chantable parts.

Share Michael's 'We're Going On A Bear Hunt'. Encourage children to join in with the words and the actions. They will be able to pick it up quickly.

Tell them that you noticed how they all seemed to be moving at the same time, and in the same way.

Get the whole class making Michael's 'beat' noise that comes in at the beginning of the video. Then, set half of the class chanting 'We're Going On A Bear Hunt, We're Gonna Catch A Big One' whilst the other half keeps the beat going.

This will help them when they have their minds blown by

the next video, which sees Michael perform it alongside the beatboxer SK Shlomo.

Watch the 'We're Going On A Bear Hunt: How To Beatbox' video.

Get the children to join in and to notice the different sounds that Shlomo creates to match Michael's words. Talk about the different bits of the poem – when is the rhythm strongest? When does the rhythm stop?

Encourage the children to create their own performances in small groups.

PART TWO

An Interview With Michael Rosen

Wednesday 2nd December 2020
Michael Rosen, Jonny Walker and Joe Rosen

Jonny   You've got a book out called *Writing For Pleasure*, and there is now a lot more talk about the idea of writing for pleasure in schools. Does poetry writing need to be pleasurable? If so, where is the pleasure?

Michael   I think that for children, ideally it should be pleasurable. I don't think it matters very much to me, and I've been writing it forever, and if it sometimes gets a bit unpleasant or frustrating, then I can put up with that because I've got this long tailback of knowing that the outcome might – if I get it right – be pleasurable. And if it doesn't, well I can chuck it away. It's much less invested in the feeling that I have, but I think with children and lower school secondary students, it should ideally be pleasurable. It is a 'Can Do' form.

If you make it so difficult or so uninvolved in the children's lives or interests, then I think we end up in a state of negativity that is very hard to overcome. It is very easy for children and young people to just go 'Well poetry is crap because I

93

didn't enjoy that lesson'. You often see it on Twitter, with people saying 'I didn't like poetry in school because . . .' and then you'll hear something like 'because we spent a long time analysing Wordsworth's 'On Westminster Bridge' and I've never read anything since'.

And I think that's a great shame. There's nothing wrong with analysing On Westminster Bridge, but if it's unpleasant and puts kids off poetry, then it's a law of negative returns.

Joe   And isn't it more dangerous than that? It also imbues a sense of failure in them as well? If it's too difficult and they don't enjoy it, somehow their self-esteem is dented in some way?

Michael   Absolutely yeah – if you blame yourself, and think 'other people can do this and I can't' then that's damaging.

Jonny   With that idea of it being a 'Can Do' form then, have you found from all those years doing poetry workshops that there are some children who are more naturally inclined towards expressing themselves through poetry than others? Does it hook in some children more easily than others?

Michael   Two things I've noticed. One is that I've noticed when a child, or a class, or a whole school has read a lot of poetry, then it's a matter of their heads being full of possibilities. It's not about nature. They've had Please Mrs. Butler, they've had Coral Rumble . . . all sorts of people that they've read, and they feel at home in it. That's one thing.

Then I sometimes notice that the children who have previously found it very difficult to write anything sometimes are liberated by the form because it appears so undemanding. If all you've got to write down is stuff that you can see, hear, think and dream, and you can perform it . . . Wow!

I've seen it work almost in the opposite direction from the repertoire point of view. For people who've never thought that they can write, suddenly a door opens and there's a room they can go into and they never knew they could go in there.

Jonny   I am immediately thinking of children I teach and have taught. In a poetry lesson there was a child who in all of the talking elements was the most vocal, extroverted and full of ideas, but as soon as it became time to write, he sidled up next to me and asked for a Writing Frame. I told him we don't need a frame, we are just jotting down ideas.

I find that because in class some children become so dependent on our teacher models, sometimes the children who are the 'strongest' in English lessons struggle most with the sort of approach we've put together in this book.

Michael   Well one of the ways to break that down is to do my daydream exercise. You just say 'daydream for 30 seconds or a minute' – however long you think they could do – and straight after the daydream, to jot down anything that they daydreamed. They don't have to write sentences. It could be single words, it could be phrases, it could be sounds. And they then look at what they've got on the page and just play with it. Try repeating bits. Maybe some parts rhyme, and maybe not. See if there's a rhythm there.

Just play with it. Move it around. If necessary you can cut it up with scissors and move the pieces around and see that. That's a way of breaking what we might call for the moment 'the tyranny of the sentence' – you aren't bound by it, and you can write in bits and pieces and play with them.

Joe   Is there something to be said for the preparatory work?

You are getting the mind ready to engage with poetry? The initial question was about does it work for some children and not others – is there something to the idea of 'getting ready to do poetry'?

Michael   Yeah. Well traditionally I've done it via poetry itself. You read a poem, talk about it and then you start playing around with the shape of it or the sound or it or the rhythm of it. But yeah absolutely. If you take my 'After Dark' poem, there aren't full sentences in a poem like that, so if you play with it, you are in a sense saying to children 'Look, you can just say 'Lights on the curtain', you don't have to say 'There are lights on the curtain.' Imagery can work like that.

But again, the daydream, the painting and the music are all quite a good way to get in a poetry mood, provided you've got this idea that you can free write. You can free write while the music is on, so you can just write single words and put them down anywhere on the page. You show them that a page doesn't have to be lines. You can show that again by looking at a painting.

Jonny   Thinking of it for teachers then – for teachers to view children's writing in this way, and for teachers to be willing to encourage the children to break the tyranny of the sentence, it will require us to hold a different way of thinking about the children's writing process.

Maybe that would be good for us to talk about now. What does it mean to be a reader of children's writing, as a teacher of poetry?

Michael   Well I think it can go on and on, developing. It's not as if you suddenly become a 'reader of children's poetry'.

What I'd say is that we used to talk – in a very 'trad' way – about literature as having the three pillars of story, drama and poetry. It was said as if it was self-evident that if you want to say that 'this country – or the world - has produced these literary forms' as a kind of cultural transmission, and that part of education is to pass on this idea. This is the wealth and richness of what literature is.

When we are asking teachers to look at their children's poetry, we're not saying it's necessary that it has to conform to great poems of the past. It was a bit like that when I was in school. We felt under the shadow of Walter de la Mare or William Shakespeare or whatever, and we could never write as well as that. If you did try, there was a faint sense of 'well . . . you are only ten".

So what I would say to teachers is that there are so many forms and shapes in poetry and some of them are absolutely ideal for six-year-olds, seven-year-olds, or ten-year-olds, to make them themselves. We don't ever have to look down on children for doing that, and what they are doing is contributing to that third pillar, poetry, which is literature.

They are doing it in their voices and at their level, and at their level of understanding and capabilities. So, all I would say to teachers is to enjoy this incredibly diverse world of poetry and see that part of it is by children's voices.

We used to publish a lot of children's poetry. It used to come out in a variety of ways. There used to be the great big Daily Mirror competitions. There was the Beever book of children's poetry. Quite a few books used to come out, and then you'd have a place like CLPE that published poetry by children every year. And it's quite hard for teachers to see books of children's poems they've written, so that they've got – I don't want to use the word – but a standard. A sense that this is the stuff that children write.

All I'd say is for teachers to see that young people's voices are valid, as voices.

Jonny   Do you think it might require some unlearning from teachers? I don't think that I had bad teacher training – I was at the IoE and I was taught helpful things about writing – but it has taken a long time into my teaching career for writing to be spoken about independently of the assessment of writing. It seems to have taken a while to get away from the question 'is this a good piece of writing?' only ever really coming up in the sense of monitoring and accountability.

Michael   Yes. Well there's two things. There's the monitoring point that you make, but also, poetry can create in some people something slightly sanctimonious and sacralised. Some people's experience of poetry in school, particularly at GCSE and A Level, and at college, is that this is a difficult, obscure, strange form, and that you the reader are not quite capable of grasping them. It's either because you're insensitive or not very intelligent.

Well this is a terrible terrible legacy of a particular form of education around poetry that happens to 15+ year olds. So instead we can see poetry as 'maybe that one doesn't work for me, but this one does', which is totally legitimate. I think that almost every day! I think 'that poem's not for me'.

Find a form you like and share it.

We don't need to bow down to all poetry, and feel sorry about ourselves that we aren't good enough for a poem, or alternatively, thinking 'Don't a lot of people waste a lot of time doing it?'. I don't have an answer to that one.

If teachers say it is a waste of time, I can justify poetry in a variety of ways, but if they really finally do believe it is a waste of time, I'm not somebody who's going to say they need to do this instead of . . . looking at snails or whatever else they'd want to do.

Jonny   Yes. OK. I guess this leads us to what I hope isn't a negative question at the end, but an interesting one. Why bother? When the role of the teacher is already so busy, why bother?

Michael   Why bother? Poetry can tell stories very well and it can describe feelings very well. It can tell quick stories, like in Humpty Dumpty, which is a brilliant little short story, as are most nursery rhymes. Poems are good storytellers. A poem can also tell things in long forms like ballads and monologues as well. But it really is very good with feelings. You can just talk your way through a feeling in a poem, and you can do it in hundreds of different ways.

On top of that, I'd say there is a linguistic point. Poetry has always played with language itself. You can go back to Chaucer, you can go back to The Odyssey – it plays with language either to make it fit forms or to play within the lines, with sounds and rhythms.

The stuff we are doing just now is chatting, but you can box it up and squeeze it, and some people call this elevated, some call it the "best words in the best order". Because it involves choice and selection, it starts to become a comment about language itself. I think this is a fantastic tool to give to children, to show them that instead of language being stuff you receive, it is the stuff in the books in your room, it is the voice of a teacher in assembly. It's all there and it belongs to everybody.

When you are writing a story to a very fixed form because it has been scaffolded and modelled and all the rest of it, you may not feel that it is yours. But if you do poetry in a very free way, then you can very quickly get to a point where children and young people can feel it is theirs. Now that is important, because it is about ownership of language. When you are owning the language and feel like you can use it to describe your world, and you in your world, then suddenly language is full of possibilities.

Instead of being a constraint, instead of being something that is imposed on you, and you are never good enough to get it in the clever way that this piece of non-fiction or fiction does, you suddenly think . . . I can do this. There's a Can Do element about the kind of poetry that I'm talking about.

Jonny   And would you say these motivations for children are the same ones that keep you writing?

Michael   If something happens to me, or I remember things, then quite often the best way I find to deal with it is to write some kind of a poem. It might sometimes be just a paragraph, it might just be what we traditionally used to call a prose poem. Or it might be something more, where I am playing around with images or playing around with rhymes and rhythms. It depends. By and large, that's the voice that I find familiar and useful.

Jonny   Would it be too much to call writing poetry a coping mechanism for life?

Michael   No, absolutely — it is one of the ways to cope. If things happen to you and they are bothersome, or even traumatic — anything along that line from itchy all the way to terrible – what do you do with it? If you have no outlet at all to express it, then what it does is sit in your head.

Again, I'll use an image. It's like an abscess in your tooth. It eats away at the flesh, around where you are first infected. Well I sometimes think that it's a bit like that if you have a bother or a trauma, it eats away in your mind, causing a kind of abscess.

If you write about it, in my experience, two things happen. You put it in an order and a shape, and that's quite satisfying in itself, because when it's in there it doesn't feel like it's got a shape. It feels tyrannical, rushing around in your brain, abscessing you. When you get it out and it's on the page, you've got it in a shape but now what you've got is something you could contemplate.

You are looking at something you've made out of that bother or trauma and then you can say 'Is that what it feels like? Wow, am I that person?"

Suddenly, you've got a triangle between you, the abscessed trauma or bother, and the thing on the page. So you've got a form of objectivity.

Sometimes there are things that have bothered me, and then I've written about it, and it's not bothering me so much. I've literally put it away, put it to bed. I've cured the abscess. You might say it's a coping mechanism but we need those don't we.

Jonny   Absolutely, and children too. It would be wonderful if an additional message from this book was that not only is writing poetry a good way to develop vocabulary and linguistic flair – it also contributes to a good life, for the children and for ourselves. A great boon.

Maybe then, as the final question . . . why do you want children and teachers to see your YouTube channel, which is the ultimate motivation for this book? What do we want from this?

Michael   I hope that teachers and children will see that it is a place full of possibilities. I want them to be entertained. I want them to be intrigued. I want them to think 'Ooh, how weird', and at other times to think, 'Brilliant!'

All those things, but also, as an overall feeling, I would like them to see what is possible.

In other words, you can say stuff and perform stuff and write stuff that is about very ordinary things, some of the time. Sometimes extraordinary, but sometimes very ordinary. And you can perform them, you can use your voice, your face, your hands and you can use these things and this is a world of possibilities. Rather than thinking of things closing down, that it is just the opposite.

You've got a landscape that you can explore, and this landscape is very various. I'm only as various as I am, but I have done some poems by other people and in other languages, as you know. It is meant to be a set of hooks, to draw teachers and children and parents and carers of all kinds in, to say 'Oh I could do something like that'. These days, with your phone all you need to do is just talk a poem to your phone and share it with someone. And so it is to enable and to show that there is this set of possibilities.

I would like them to see what is possible.

Appendix

The Elements of Children's Social Culture in the 2020s

Michael's 1988 classic *Did I Hear You Write?* included an article titled 'Young People, Culture and the School', as well as a list of the features of young people's culture. In the article, he defines culture loosely as 'the way people carry out their affairs together', and suggests it has origins in the relationships between a person, their family, their friend and peer groups, and their national, cultural, ethnic or class groups (depending on how they self-define, or how others define them).

Michael's point was that there are certain topics and activities which pull together all these elements of children's cultural selves, and that these often are overlooked by schools. He suggests these might be met with 'a combination of ignorance, indifference, contempt or hostility'. He gives the example of four black teenage boys 'toasting', improvising lyrics over a Sugar Minott dub beat in the style of Yellowman.

What might today's equivalents be? In terms of music, grime remains outside most schools' orbit, despite rap having become part of the cultural mainstream. Jeffrey Boakye writes brilliantly about this in *Hold Tight: Black Masculinity, Millennials and the Meaning of Grime* – 'black culture (and its various offshoots) is the dominant youth culture'. Explaining what excites him so much about grime and why he thinks it is so popular with his students, Boakye suggests 'its energy, wit, underlying social protest and unashamed Britishness make it a compelling incarnation for UK youth culture'.

Think of the different things we've explored in this book to help children and young people to write authentically – rich conversation, playfulness with language, humour, pride in our own experiences, writing as we speak, truth-telling, social consciousness – and you can find it embodied in grime.

The internet has globalised culture. In the last few decades, the world's floodgates of music, film, TV and video have opened. Today's British kids can and do engage with Japanese animé, South Korean pop music, and American TV online. YouTube and other video sharing apps like TikTok mean that within a few hours, children and young people from around the world may all be consuming the same content – a song, a dance, a clip, a joke, a prank, a phrase, a meme, a Michael Rosen poetry video!

Gaming is another transformed element – for many children and young people, gaming isn't so much something they do as it is a part of who they are. Through gaming, they interact with family and friends, they develop their own language and gain a different sense of self.

If we really mean it when we say we want children to write authentically, then we need to invite this into the classroom. That doesn't mean we need to sack off Science lessons in order to play Fortnite – it means that we need to recognise the significance of children's worlds outside the classroom in order to understand them better when they are in it.

I return to Michael's original article regularly when planning and teaching poetry and creative writing sessions for children and young people of all ages. I find his list of the 'components of any young person's culture' to be a helpful tool in a poetry classroom.

Discussing these things can lead to poems – as is the focus here – but also oral histories, proverbs, cartoons, life histories, anecdotes, documentaries, monologues, playscripts, stand-up comedy routines, podcasts and so many other forms.

Perhaps when you see this list, you will think that there are some missing elements. Children's youth cultures are always shifting and changing, and that is part of what makes the language so rich. You might want to add some categories yourself – do let us know on Twitter too.

Perhaps in your class you could make a Word Wall. This can be a large display where the children can bring words, phrases, sayings, snatches of songs, poems, street names – anything that catches their eye or ear. They could categorise what they collect, using headings from the following 'culture' list. The Word Wall is for sharing but they could do the same in a notebook to make more private lists.

Our fears	Dreams and nightmares	Playing tricks
Getting revenge	People we trust	Thrills
Getting in trouble	Accidents and injuries	Things we regret
The feeling of pride	The feeling of shame	Unexplained mysteries

Vows and resolutions	Wishes and hopes	Rumours and gossip
Proverbs	Rhymes	Games
What we are reading	What we are listening to	What we are watching
Breaking the law	Formal rules	Unwritten rules
Punishment	Sayings	Stories we have been told
Special events in my culture	The history of my culture	Stories from my language and culture
Things my family understand about me	Things my family don't understand about me	What I do to relax
Jokes	Songs	Unexpected events
Feelings about family	Conversations with family	Making each other laugh
Places we go to hang out	Celebrations	Feasts
Favourite meals	The best food we've tasted	The worst food we've tasted
Fashion	Hairstyles	Trainers
Hobbies	Crazes	Viral trends

Music we listen to	Dance routines	Music we perform
Sports we watch	Sports we play	Playground sport
Having a job	What our family do for work	Not having a job
Online gaming chat	Who does and doesn't play	Being banned from technology
Chores and housework	Our own bedrooms	Relationships
Getting married	Getting divorced	Single parenthood
Gay parenthood	Being gay, lesbian and/or bisexual	Being transgender/ non-binary
Going on holiday	Day trips	School trips
Slang	Local dialect	Secret languages
Gaming talk	Language from memes	YouTube terms
Local news and drama	Street spectacles and events	Superstitions
Being famous	Having followers online	Being a YouTuber
Keeping secrets	Well-known local people	Local stories and urban legends
Fairness	Cheating	What makes us laugh

Heroes and villains	Scapegoats	Being a victim
Privacy	Things that annoy us	Body image
Beauty standards	Taking sides in disputes	Being caught between cultures
Fights and violence	Gangs	Drugs
Gender differences	Gender inequalities	Gender stereotypes
Having a phone	Being on social media	Having Whatsapp/ Snapchat
Social change	The future for me	The future for all of us
Climate change	Death	Life after death
God	Religious differences	Struggles with faith
Importance of religion	Disasters	My space – my room, my home
Fantasies	Daydreams	Odd thoughts
Friendships	Losing friendships	Being popular
Being unpopular	Being cool	Being uncool
Love	Dating	Romance

Fancying people	Solidarity	Sticking up for friends
Pretending to be something you're not	Teachers having favourites	The imagined private lives of teachers
School gossip	Community gossip	Neighbours
Unusual weather	Pets	Parties
Encountering strangers	Getting into arguments	Dealing with conflict
Anger	Racism	Politics
Being disappointed	Making promises	Breaking promises
Mood changes	Things I care about	Things I don't care about

Acknowledgements

Thanks to Sam Creighton, Tasneem Ahmed, Nikki Gamble and Charlotte Raby, whose questions, corrections and suggestions helped to improve early drafts. Thanks to Ross Young and Felicity Ferguson for fine-tuning the final draft and for knowing and sharing all of their encyclopaedic research into how to teach writing.

Thanks to Farzana Hussain, Natasha Ttoffali and Sukwinder Samra, three brilliant headteachers who have supported me since I started teaching. I am very thankful for your leadership, friendship and nurture.

Thanks too to Adisa the Verbaliser, my partner-in-rhyme on poetry retreats. I remain in awe of how you develop children's play, lyricism and consciousness with such a light touch.

Special thanks to the children at Glade Primary School, where I have been trying out lots of the mini-lessons in this book – your humour, conversation and creativity are the reason why teaching you is such a fun and hopeful thing to do with my time.

Thanks to the hundreds of online colleagues who have joined in with conversations on Twitter about this book, using the #MiRoPoViBo hashtag. Michael and I cannot wait to see how you and your children get along with the book, and we'd love to see what you create together.

Thanks to Joe Rosen, for our Zooms throughout the writing process. I have really enjoyed our talks, and your expertise and questioning have helped massively.

And finally, I'd like to thank Michael Rosen for inviting me to write this book with him – it has been a pleasure to spend so much time immersed in the wisdom and warmth of your words.

Related Books by Michael Rosen

POETRY AND STORIES
FOR PRIMARY AND LOWER
SECONDARY SCHOOLS

MICHAEL ROSEN

This is a short guide for teachers on how to teach poetry – reading, responding and writing. It is full of ideas on where and how to start, descriptions of why it's such a valuable activity. It's for you to use, adapt and change as you think best for the school and students you have in front of you.

WHY WRITE?
WHY READ?

MICHAEL ROSEN

This booklet gathers together some recent talks and blogs on writing and reading, for use by teachers, librarians, parents, or anyone interested in engaging children and students in reading, writing, analysing why and how we do both.

This booklet is third in a series about reading, writing and responding to literature. It focusses on how to make writing pleasurable and interesting and would be ideal as part of teacher training, staff discussion, curriculum development or just reading and using.

This is a short guide for teachers on how to help a school put in place a reading for pleasure policy. To support this policy the guide also takes a close look at how children read — what do they think as they read? I've also included some plans from teachers putting reading for pleasure policies in place. It's for you to use, adapt and change as you think best for the school and students you have in front of you.

Lightning Source UK Ltd.
Milton Keynes UK
UKHW010630010421
381372UK00001B/350